THE COMPLETE BOOK OF SEMINOLE PATCHWORK

Beverly Rush
with
Lassie Wittman

DOVER PUBLICATIONS, INC.
New York

Dedicated to the memory of the early Seminole women, who developed an ingenuous beauty in the midst of great hardship, and of Flo Wilson Campbell, who brought a fresh outlook to their work.

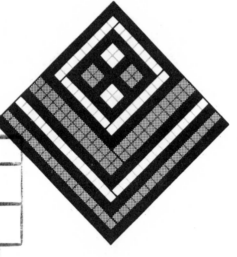

Bibliographical Note

This Dover edition, first published in 1993, is a republication of *The Complete Book of Seminole Patchwork: From Traditional Methods to Contemporary Uses*, originally published by Madrona Publishers, Inc., Seattle, Washington, in 1982. The book has been reset and reformatted, and the original color section has been omitted. Many of the photographs originally found in the color section have been reproduced in color on the covers.

Library of Congress Cataloging-in-Publication Data

Rush, Beverly.
   The complete book of Seminole patchwork / Beverly Rush with Lassie Wittman.
      p.   cm. — (Dover needlework series)
   Previously published: Seattle, WA : Madrona Publishers, 1982.
(Reset and reformatted, with original color section omitted)
   Includes bibliographical references and index.
   ISBN 0-486-27617-1
   1. Patchwork. 2. Quilting. 3. Seminole Indians—Costume and adornment. 4. Seminole Indians—Textile industry and fabrics. I. Wittman, Lassie. II. Title. III. Series.
TT835.R87 1993
746.9′2—dc20
                                  93-29549
                                    CIP

Manufactured in the United States of America
Dover Publications, Inc., 31 East 2nd Street, Mineola, N.Y. 11501

Acknowledgments

Lassie and I wish to acknowledge the special help and encouragement given by so many: the Unorganized Stitchers, Gerry Machovec, Dorothy Downs, Karen Johanson, Barbara Chasan, Marlene Rossi, Jacqueline Enthoven, Carol Wiegel, Judybill Osceola, Rosa Billie, and every artist whose work is shown, especially the Indian women who invited either Lassie or me into their homes.

We are especially grateful to three historians who read and gave advice on parts of the manuscript: J. Floyd Monk, member of the Florida Historical Society; Dr. John L. Oldani, Director of the Folklore and Quilt Archive, Southern Illinois University at Edwardsville, Edwardsville, Illinois; and Dr. Charlton W. Tebeau, author of *Man in the Everglades: 2000 Years of Human History in the Everglades National Park*, University of Miami Press, 1964.

Contents

Introduction

As my interest in stitchery deepened in the 1960s to include teaching and writing, I remembered childhood studies of the Seminole Indians and their bright clothing. With each of my two books, *Stitch with Style* (Madrona Publishers, 1979) and *The Stitchery Idea Book* (Van Nostrand Reinhold, 1974), I added to my research; but the subject merited more attention than a short account in a general book. Over the years I investigated museums and private collections, talked to numerous knowledgeable specialists, and visited reservations in Florida. I visited Indian women in their homes, sometimes with an interpreter. I saw how they worked, met their children, saw where their work was sold.

What we know as Seminole patchwork was developed by the Mikasuki-speaking Seminole Indian women of southern Florida around the end of the 1800s. Despite what is often assumed about Indian art, their work is mostly not symbolic—it is also not ancient and not primitive. From an earlier, simpler appliqué, these women developed a structural patchwork by joining strips of cloth lengthwise into long, multicolored bands, cutting these bands into segments, and assembling the segments in a preplanned order into long bands of geometric pattern. These, in turn, were cut and joined with each other and with plain strips of fabric to make material for garments. Clothing was cut so that these crayon-bright patterns always ran in horizontal rows. This colorful apparel has become the hallmark and the most visible art form of the Seminole culture.

While simple in concept, the technique for constructing Seminole patterns allows many design possibilities and variations. There are about three hundred patterns diagramed in this book, all adapted from patterns seen in use by Seminole women unless otherwise noted.

As always, sharing interests with good friends—some new, some old—made every bit of research rewarding. Flo Wilson Campbell went with me to Phoenix, where we took notes and photographed, diagramed, and sketched examples in the collection of the Heard Museum, thanks to Patrick T. Houlihan, the museum's director, and Jane Kauffman, who made arrangements. In Florida I stayed with, and was organized by, Gerry Machovec, whose intense interest in Indian cultures stems from her newspaper days in Los Alamos, New Mexico. She introduced me to Patsy West, then at the Historical Museum of Southern Florida, who guided my research in the museum's files

Fig. 1. *Seminole patchwork sampler, 34 by 41 inches (86 by 104 cm). Commissioned from Annie C. Billie by Wayne Rogers for author.*

and showed an enthusiastic interest in my photographs of contemporary work. Gerry arranged to have Dorothy Downs join us on our visit to the Big Cypress Reservation. Dot was then doing research on Indian medicine pouches and has since written fine articles about Florida Indian clothing: one for the Lowe Art Museum catalog of the exhibition The Art of the Florida Indian, which she was instrumental in organizing, one for the *American Indian Art Magazine* (Summer, 1979). Gerry not only took photographs on those visits; she also took notes as I chatted with the women about their patchwork.

Early in the research, I shared my excitement over Seminole patchwork with a group of northwestern stitchers that both Flo and I were a part of, a group called the Unorganized Stitchers. Brought together by Jacqueline Enthoven in 1969, this group has been meeting ever since. Its interest, too, was caught by the possibilities of the Seminole technique. Lassie Witt-

Fig. 2. *Seminole man's shirt, circa 1930. From the collection of the Heard Museum, Phoenix.*

Fig. 3. *Apron showing larger patterns typical of the 1940s. From the collection of Barbara Schroeder.*

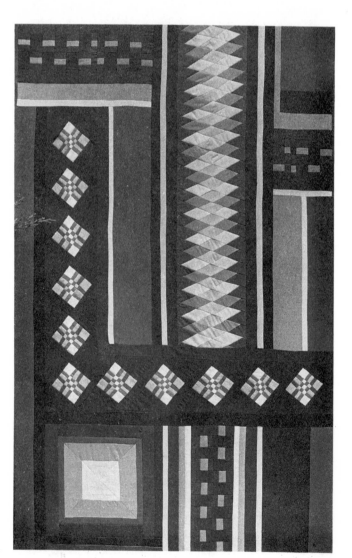

man was especially enthusiastic and soon was researching and producing new ideas of her own, becoming one of the country's foremost teachers of Seminole patchwork. Her own research has taken her to Florida three times, and she counts several of the Indian women artists as her friends. Lassie wrote and self-published a good, small manual on this technique but found she prefers teaching to writing. From the start Lassie promised some help on this book; I was totally delighted when she agreed to participate fully.

Some of the most exciting contemporary work built on Seminole technique was done by Flo Wilson Campbell. Our visit to the Heard Museum was her first exposure to patchwork. Within a few months I was taking notes on what *she* was doing! Building on the Indian concepts, she was freely using the bands and strips in new ways. It was her idea that the Unorganized Stitchers coordinate their efforts in a group project. Twelve wall panels were individually designed and made; the fabrics were the same in each. These were sold as a group, and today they hang throughout a Tacoma doctor's office. A second group

Fig. 4. *Mounted panel, 24 by 48 inches (61 by 122 cm). By Pat Albiston, who used Seminole techniques for a contemporary design.*

2

project was designed and organized by Eleanor Van de Water and was shown in Needle Expressions '80, the semiannual national exhibition sponsored by the National Standards Council of American Embroiderers. This project consists of modular units that can be hung in a variety of combinations. Photos of both projects appear in the book. Flo actively worked on her patchwork art until her death in 1976.

We Unorganized Stitchers in the Northwest feel a special kinship to the Indian women of the Southeast. We, too, have enjoyed working together, yet individually, inspired by their invention. Today their influence, both direct and indirect, can be seen in patchwork and quilting all over the United States. They deserve full credit for their contribution.

Fig. 5. Seminole-made skirt of nontypical colors. The skirt is light beige, and the patterns use rust, blues, and turquoise. Bought by Happy Leight at a national square-dance festival in 1968.

Fig. 7. Apron made by Annie Jim, Miccosukee. The colors are unusual—white, with a pattern band of white and navy and with red and green details.

Fig. 6. Skirt made by Mary Motlow. From the collection of the author.

Fig. 8. Seminole tea aprons made for tourists.

Basics

Basic Concept of Seminole Patchwork

Seminole patchwork differs from most American patchwork in its construction as well as its appearance. It is made by sewing torn strips of fabric into long multicolored bands. The bands are then cut into segments that are arranged and joined together in geometric designs.

The Seminole women were not the first to use a strip method. Joining strips of fabric, then cutting and rejoining the resulting bands in different directions was practiced by the American colonists. Dot Moye has a quilt in her collection made by her grandmother in 1866 in South Carolina that uses a strip method of

Fig. 10. *Patchwork skirt purchased from the Seminoles and remade to a non-Indian style by Barbara Schroeder. Bought in 1944, the patchwork is exceptionally fine workmanship.*

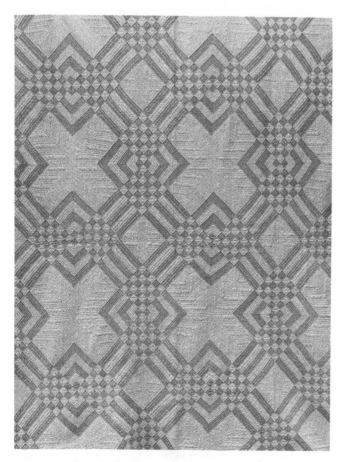

Fig. 9. *Quilt made by Ellen Alford Boney of North Carolina in 1866, of calico and unginned cotton batting. Areas of squares were cut from long strips and flipped for checkerboard effect, a technique the Florida Indians came to use. Owned by Dorothy Moye, Ellen Boney's great-granddaughter.*

piecing (*Fig. 9*). The strips were left uncut for part of the design, but they were also cut and rejoined for the checkerboard areas in the same way Seminole bands are used. Southern slaves (many of whom ran away and lived with the Seminoles, some of them intermarrying) were known for their "strippy" quilts, in which they pieced long strips of cloth into linear designs, many showing African influences.

However, a strip method of piecing fabric was not the colonists' most common patchwork technique. Most of their patchwork was in quilts, and the cloth for these quilts was usually made of scraps of clothing or leftover pieces of fabric joined, padded, and quilted. Quilting for the colonists was mainly a way of reusing, or using up, bits and scraps, to cover the bed. So colonial designs reflect a technique of pieces fitted and joined one at a time.

Seminole women used new fabric to make patch-

Fig. 11. Skirt purchased more recently. From the collection of Lassie Wittman.

Fig. 12. Seminole apron with three bands. Most tourist aprons have fewer bands.

work for clothing—pieced but not quilted. Their designs show a geometric repetition and precision unique to the cut-and-joined-band method. In general, they chose bright colors and used color combinations of a vibrance that would have shocked the conservative colonists.

While not the first to use the strip method, the Seminoles were the first to carry its possibilities to the design dimension now found in their work.

The work appears more complex than it actually is. In an article for the *Antiques Journal* (October, 1975), writer Betty Evanoff notes, "Some of the designs require as many as nine one-inch pieces of fabric to make one small inset and thus, a long skirt can easily contain over 4,000 pieces." Some patterns contain squares much smaller than the one-inch size Evanoff mentions. But the efficiency of the method is such that a pattern made up of nine squares can be accomplished by cutting and resewing only two bands, each made up of three strips of cloth. Never once are the smallest pieces handled individually. As beautifully intricate as Seminole patchwork appears, its basic construction is beautifully simple and is a unique contribution to the general art of patchwork.

While the technique is efficient as well as ingenious, doing Seminole patchwork well takes time and patience, as does any sewing or any art. Take the time to understand the underlying structure of the patchwork, and you will not only be able to analyze and construct any pattern you see, but you'll be able to invent countless new ones of your own.

Color—Traditional and Contemporary

Every era, every culture, has its color signature, influenced by a diversity of factors. In the color of clothing, these factors include fibers and dyes indigenous to a culture and those acquired through trade or import. The technology of fibers, weaves, dyes—and the transportation to spread this technology—creates possibilities or sets limits to fabric and color development anywhere.

Most of us usually think of "Indian colors" as the colors of the earth: siennas, ochres, beiges, and blacks. The dress shown in *color plate A* has Seminole patterns made in rust, blue, white, black, and brown— set in a beige dress fabric. I repeatedly hear comments about it being in the "real" colors. It isn't.

If there is one overwhelming impression when seeing the Florida Indians in their traditional dress, it is in response to the vibrancy of color. Clear-color mosaics dance with every motion. The clothes are happy clothes, suggesting the freedom and joy of a carnival or a carousel's colorful whirling movement; yet they are worn by a shy and reserved people, as though the clothes reach out, while the people pull back and go quietly about their day.

The bright, clear colors are often set against black. Bright reds, yellows, and a fresh turquoise are favorite colors in the traditional patchwork. Even when pinks or browns are used, they are not softened but are the colors found full strength in a paintbox. Thus, if you want your patterns to take on a "Seminole look," you

Fig. 13. Modern man's black jacket with multicolored bands.

Fig. 14. Strip-pieced angles and values of only two color families form pattern. By Jean Affleck.

will need to use these same kinds of colors. Most likely, however, you will want to find the color combinations that fit you or match your wardrobe.

I find it impossible to look at the paintings of Victor Vasarely without immediately getting new ideas for Seminole. I even keep feeling that if he had known about the Seminoles' work when he was a younger man, he would have enjoyed it tremendously. In his own work he wanted to produce that which everyone, not just the rich, could enjoy; and further, he wanted to produce work that others—not just that rarefied creature, the artist—could also learn to produce. He loved geometrics and wanted his work to fit the technological age. He would have delighted in the Indians' use of the sewing machine. His color schemes are highly sophisticated and complicated; yet they give an impression of clear, often primary, colors—and they are frequently set off against black. His geometrics become form, show motion, and create planes that play with the eye through optical illusions.

All these effects are possible, to some extent, with Seminole technique; some areas of colors can be made to float, others to advance or recede, by the combination of pattern and color. It is especially effective to use your background color to carry through as one of the colors within the pattern. This can create the effect that parts of the pattern are floating in space; only the areas *other* than the background color seem to be there. Your library will have several books on Vasarely; find color plates of his work and enjoy them with Seminole patchwork in mind.

Color is associative; color has fashion. Margaret Walch, who wrote the *Color Source Book* (Charles Scribner's Sons, 1979), gives color swatches of the color palettes associated with forty-eight periods, cultures, and artists. She shows color signatures found in Chinese porcelains, Coptic textiles, Persian carpets, Greek pottery, Wedgwood china, Gauguin and El Greco paintings, Tiffany glass, pop art, and Sheila Hicks's fiber art. Carol Thrailkill matched the colors shown for every palette to Paternayan yarns, which she wound around cards—one card holding all of the colors given within one palette—and filed for future ideas and reference.

Cloth can be wound around cards also. Examples of color ideas recorded in this way can be seen in *Fig. 16*. When you make your own color records, the colors on the printed page and those of your fabrics may not match perfectly. Lassie put together a set of color combinations she liked from a book about Navajo rugs. Her colors are consistently brighter than those in the Indian rugs because the cotton-blend fabrics she works with are not beautifully faded, as are the old rugs, and because a color in flat weave has a different appearance than it has in heavier handweaving. Though the colors don't match perfectly, they guided her to some beautiful combinations, new to her work.

To make your own color samples, use pieces of cardboard the size of bias tape packages. Select the fabrics you want to use and cut your samples, which only need to be an inch or so wide (or a convenient 2.5 cm) and just long enough to go around the cardboard.

Fig. 15. Blue Stripes, *72 by 108 inches (183 by 274 cm), a strip-pieced wall quilt made by Donna Prichard. The design is established entirely by the value range within a limited color palette.*

Fig. 17. Lassie Wittman shown marking a band, using a transparent grid ruler and soap.

Fig. 16. Tools and supplies. Color-wrapped cards can be used to record and file color combinations.

Lay out the fabric strips with edges overlapping to approximately repeat the positions and proportions of color shown in the example you're working from. When you're satisfied with a piece of fabric, tape it into position onto the cardboard. (Tape the pieces one at a time, as you select them; they move around too much to be done all at once. Readjust them later, if necessary.) When taping, fold under each overlapping edge. This looks more like the seams of finished work than do the slightly softer, feathered torn edges. Mark the source of your inspiration on the back of the cardboard; later you may wish to refer to that source again.

As you work out a particular arrangement of colors, you may want to vary the original arrangement or proportions. If you do, you will want to make more than one card of the same basic color idea. With these

cards, you can easily and quickly see which color schemes you prefer, and if you save them, you will have color notes for future work.

Color Value

More important than the particular colors chosen is the placement of color values. Entire pattern shapes recede or become dominant, depending upon the intensity of their color values. A pattern plan of cut paper, or one on graph paper, should be done in gray tones or tone values of a single color; thus, any color scheme can be used for that plan by duplicating its value placements. Values of the surrounding fabric also will tremendously influence the appearance of a pattern.

Work with value to make your patterns look like the patterns diagramed in this book. Choose your own colors, but follow the example's placement of values. Color contrast is different from value contrast. A pattern might be successful in a strong color contrast of bright red and green even though it has no value contrast. But if you use a dark value or strong color where a medium or light contrast is indicated in a diagram, you might find that an entirely different shape is becoming dominant in your pattern or that you are losing a clearly defined shape, letting areas of color seem unrelated.

Within each structural pattern or seam arrangement of Seminole patchwork, innumerable color variations are possible. We have diagramed every variation we have seen the Indian women make; you can go from here.

Terms

If directions or descriptions are to be understood, certain terms must be defined. There are no official definitions of the terms used in discussing Seminole patchwork. You will find variation between individual authors and teachers. Lassie and I prefer the following explanations.

Strip: a single piece of fabric usually torn or cut from selvedge to selvedge.

Band: two or more strips sewn together along the torn or cut edges. A band may be any length as long as the color of each strip is continuous.

Segment: a small piece made by cutting across the full width of the band.

Pattern, Pattern Unit, or Design Unit: a single design motif formed by cutting and assembling segments from one or more bands.

Pattern Band: a long band of one repeated pattern.

Spacers or Insertions: a single strip, full band width, to be cut and then sewn between pattern units or segments.

Extensions or Surrounds: fabric sewn beyond the pattern unit to extend or enclose it, thus making the pattern unit a part of a larger unit. These extensions may be pieced together by methods other than the Seminole method; one such method might be the traditional log cabin technique.

Seminole Method: a patchwork technique consisting of sewing torn strips into a band, then cutting segments from the band and arranging and sewing them into geometric designs.

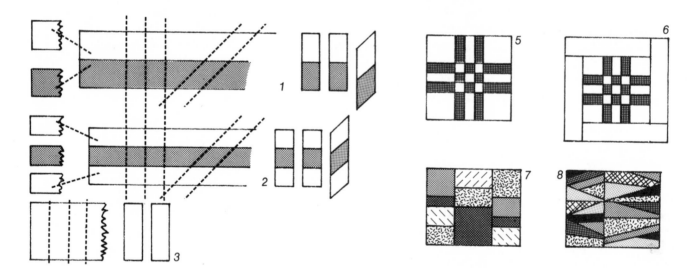

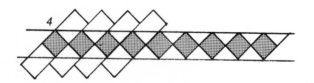

Fig. 18. Illustrations of Terms:

1. Two-strip band and segments cut from it.
2. Three-strip band and segments.
3. Plain strip cut for spacers.
4. Pattern band, a running repeat of one pattern.
5. Seminole pattern unit.
6. Seminole pattern unit with extensions added by log-cabin technique.
7. Strip method of piecing.
8. String method of piecing for quilting.

Seminole Patterns: the geometric designs produced by the Seminole method.

Strip Method: a patchwork method of joining straight-grain strips to form a vertical or horizontal area of pieced cloth. When shapes cut from this are joined, it creates a somewhat random-appearing linear design, rather than the controlled geometric patterns of the Seminole method.

String Quilting: a random joining of strips or long pieces of cloth that are not necessarily cut on the straight of the grain or in rectangles. These are "usually pieced to a foundation of fabric or of paper (which is later torn away) so that any strings sewn off-grain are not stretched or distorted," according to Robbie and Tony Fanning in *The Complete Book of Machine Quilting* (Chilton, 1980).

Tools

Seminole patchwork is, and has always been, sewn by machine. Tools should help in two ways: to make your work more precise, and to make it more efficient.

High-quality, beautiful workmanship is characterized by seams that meet where they should, by segments that line up precisely, and by design lines that run true and straight. This involves measuring and marking.

You will need a straightedge for marking lines; a clear plastic ruler marked with grids, such as those made by the C-Thru Ruler Company, works well. The C-Thru 2-by-12-inch ruler marked with ⅛-inch grids is a favorite. The grid markings can be lined up directly over a stitching line, or a marked line, for marking either parallel or perpendicular lines. A plastic triangle is also convenient for marking angles or perpendicular lines. A yardstick and a 14-by-24-inch (36-by-61-cm) carpenter's square can be helpful, especially for large-scale work.

Whatever marker you use should produce a very fine line to assure accuracy. Lassie has long recommended a sharp sliver of soap as an ideal marker—edges can be resharpened easily with a paring knife. (Make sure the soap is thoroughly dry.) A sharp pencil will do if its mark can be covered with stitching so that it does not show. Or one of the water-erasable embroidery and dressmaker's markers now on the market can be used.

Stitching is done completely by machine. Use a fine needle and eleven to thirteen stitches per inch (or for every 2.5 cm). Indian women use one color of thread for all sewing done at one time, a practical approach. You might want to select one color for the top thread and another for the bobbin, and if you are willing to

spend the needed time, you can change thread to match each change of fabric color.

Where to Start: One-Band Patterns and Paper Play

Any pattern with segments cut from only one band is a one-band pattern, but that one band may have any number of strips. A two-band pattern contains segments cut from two bands that contain different

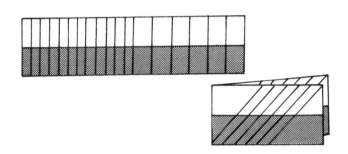

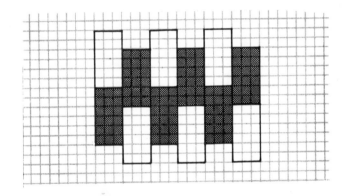

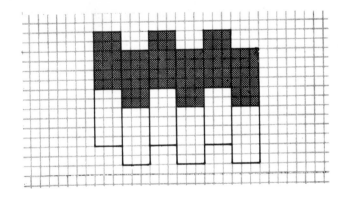

Fig. 19. *Working with colored paper is a good way to get the feel of Seminole patchwork. The drawings above show light and dark paper strips taped and marked for cutting into straight segments (top), and folded and marked for angled segments (above, right). These segments can be arranged and rearranged to explore various ways of forming patterns.*

9

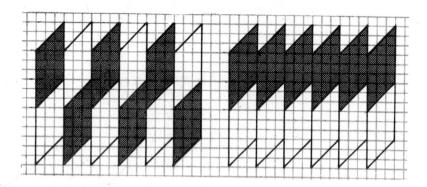

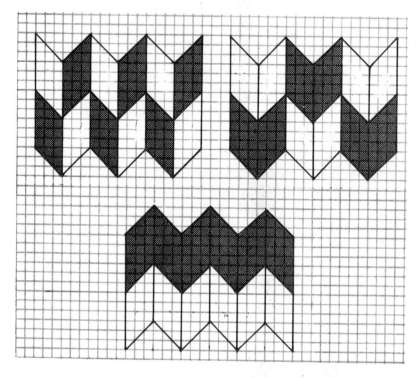

Fig. 20. *These are repeating patterns, each made of one two-strip band with segments cut in equal sizes. The angle segments above are cut in the same direction; the angle segments below are cut in two directions. The amount of fabric trimmed from the outside edges can greatly change a pattern's look.*

numbers, colors, or arrangements of strips. When we state the number of bands required for a project, the number refers to how many different bands are needed to make the design, not the number of lengths of identical bands.

The first step in doing Seminole patchwork yourself is to understand how the system works; then you will be able to make any of the traditional patterns or to come up with ideas of your own. It's helpful to start with paper, and I show Lassie's method, which she uses with her classes. You can also, and probably will want to, experiment directly with cloth and note ideas on graph paper.

In teaching, Lassie has found that the quickest way to help students learn the Seminole method is to get them cutting and playing with paper. Doing this, the students can easily understand the underlying principle of the patchwork and see how easy it is to manipulate cut bands into a profusion of patterns.

For this paper play, colors are kept monochromatic—either two shades of gray plus black and white

or four values, light to dark, of one color. The transition from paper to fabric is easier if not limited or influenced by colors.

Collect your supplies: four 9-by-12-inch (23-by-30-cm)* sheets of construction paper (four tones of one color), paper scissors, pencil, transparent tape, transparent grid ruler. A plastic triangle is helpful, and a pad of graph paper is good for recording patterns you like.

From each of two sheets of the paper, one dark, one light, cut a 1½-inch (4 cm) strip the full 12-inch (30 cm) width. Tape the strips together horizontally, running the tape along the full cut; leave no gaps. Turn the taped strips over; you now have a two-strip band that measures 3 by 12 inches (8 by 30 cm). Starting at the left edge, mark cutting lines for twelve ½-inch (1.3-cm) segments and six 1-inch (2.5-cm) segments, making sure that all lines are exactly perpendicular (at right

*Throughout the book, metric measurements with an asterisk are for convenience and are not direct equivalents of inches.

10

Six patterns made from paper, cut and taped, by Karen Johanson

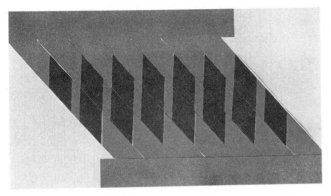

Fig. 21. *One band of five strips, cut on the diagonal.*

Fig. 24. *Two bands, one four-strip and one three-strip, alternated and set at an angle.*

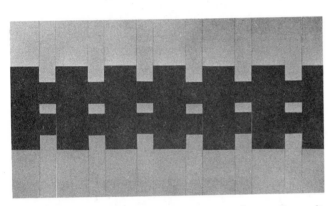

Fig. 22. *Two bands, one three-strip and one five-strip, alternated.*

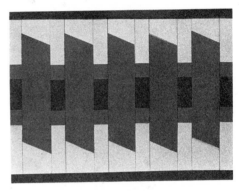

Fig. 25. *Two bands, one five-strip and one three-strip. The second band, band B, has been cut at an angle but joined straight, in line with band A.*

Fig. 23. *Exploration with one four-strip band, cut both straight and at angles.*

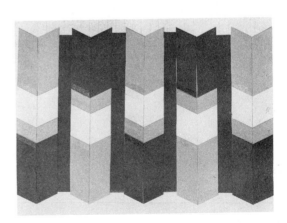

Fig. 26. *One band of four strips, cut at an angle but set with dark strips alternating top and bottom and separated by spacers.*

11

angles to the bottom). Cut into segments and stack to one side.

From the same sheets of paper, prepare a second band, identical to the first. Mark one vertical line exactly at the center of the band; to the right of this center line, mark a 45-degree diagonal. Using the transparent grid ruler and moving right, mark five more lines, parallel to the first, ½ inch (1.3 cm) apart. Lassie suggests to her classes that they mark a dot on the lighter paper between each parallel line. Later these dots will identify the right segments. The unmarked ones will be the left segments. Fold the band in half at the marked vertical with the taped sides

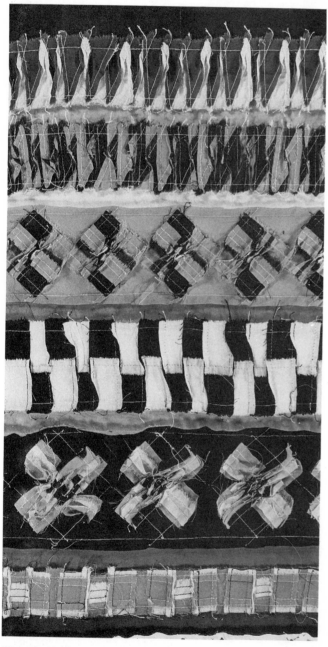

Fig. 27. *Wrong side of the Indian-made sampler shown in Fig. 1. Sewing sequence can be analyzed by the position of the cut or torn edges.*

on the inside. Crease the fold sharply, then cut along the angled lines. This gives you ten angled segments, five angled in one direction, five in the other. This is an important cutting technique and is used in many of the patterns. Put the right segments in one pile and the left segments in another.

Had you been working with fabric, you could have made all of these cuts, and then some, from one sewn band 45 inches (114 cm) long. *On cloth, however, you must add seam allowance to each cut edge.*

You now have four stacks of cut segments: straight cuts of two sizes and angled cuts of two directions, plus three leftover triangles. Set the triangles aside for later use, and arrange and rearrange your paper segments to see how many patterns you can come up with. Try to make all, or most, of the two- and three-strip running patterns shown in the diagram section. Proportions will differ slightly because different measurements are used. The segment sizes for paper play are adapted to sizes that will fit the paper rather than to modules as shown in the diagrams. In the diagrams, fractional measurements are avoided.

Figs. 21–26 show paper patterns made by Karen Johanson, who diagramed all the patterns for this book. For these paper patterns, she has used bands of more than two strips. After experimenting with two-strip paper bands, many students choose to make bands of three strips before going on to fabric. For three-strip bands, Lassie suggests 1½-inch (4 cm) strips of black and gray and a ¾-inch (2 cm) center strip of white, all cut the full 12-inch (30-cm) width of the paper and taped together as before. Perpendicularly cut segments are cut ¾ inch (2 cm) wide and the parallel angle lines are ¾ inch (2 cm) apart.

Now experiment with these segments. Try some patterns that include one or more of the leftover triangles. *Sketch any patterns you want to remember so that you can repeat them later, in fabric.*

To Tear or Not to Tear!

Strips of fabric to be used for a pattern can be torn or cut, selvedge to selvedge, across the fabric. Clip through or trim off selvedges before tearing. Some quilters do prefer lengthwise cuts—these must be cuts, as fabric does not tear well lengthwise. Six inches (15 cm) of 45-inch (114 cm) fabric will provide two 3-by-45-inch (7.6-by-114-cm) strips if cut crosswise, but cut lengthwise a 45-inch (114-cm) strip will take a 45-inch (114-cm) length of fabric, or will require many seams. However, cutting lengthwise might prove efficient if great numbers of strips are to be cut. Choose your method according to your project and your supplies. All references in this book assume crosswise tears or cuts.

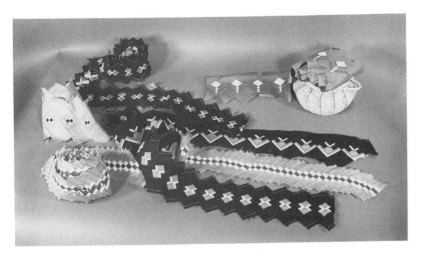

Fig. 28. Lengths cut from very long Indian-made bands. Such bands are made ahead of need, ready to be included in many garments.

Traditionally, Indian women worked with fabrics of 100 percent cotton, which could be readily torn. Segments were then cut with long, sharp scissors. Today, both cotton and cotton blends (usually cotton with polyester) are used. (Additional fabrics are discussed in "Contemporary Work.") As the percentage of polyester in a blend increases, so does the fabric's tendency to pull warp threads if torn. Blends of up to 65 percent polyester will usually tear well. If the fabric frays excessively or doesn't tear well or pulls the warp threads when you tear it, than use sharp scissors along a carefully marked line that is straight with the grain. (For her narrow strips, Annie Jim of the Tamiami Trail tears strips twice the width she wants, then rapidly scissors them straight along the center.) Accuracy is extremely important, whether cutting or tearing.

After tearing, press your strips so that they regain their natural straightness. Indian women finger-press, or they hold each strip tautly and pull it back and forth against a table edge a few times. But you'll find that a warm iron, and maybe a light spray of starch, will add just enough body to the strip to help keep seams from puckering.

Even if you prefer to cut most of the time or with most fabrics, do make up one pattern using torn fabrics. Enjoy the sensation of that fast r-r-ripping feel and sound, and think of the Indian woman sitting in her chickee, in front of her machine, tearing strip after strip of bright colors. Flo Wilson Campbell was so intrigued by the feathered edges created by tearing that she designed an entire piece to feature those edges (*color plate Q*).

Bands

Tear all the strips you need for your planned band; then sew them together along the tears. Your pattern may call for several bands. After sewing, press all the seams on a single band so that they go the same direction. If you have more than one band, press all seams on band one down, on band two up, and so forth. This makes joinings of multiple seam lines less bulky. With some fabric combinations you may want to press dark seam allowances under the darkest fabric, regardless of direction, to prevent see-through.

To make their many-yards-long bands, Indian women join the end of one torn strip to another before sewing the strips into bands. These long strips are then joined to make a band perhaps thirty yards (about twenty-nine meters) long. Since fabric widths may vary, seams where the strips have been lengthened may not line up exactly, but this is no problem. (Patterns made from these bands characteristically

Fig. 29. Variety of Indian-made bands collected by author and Lassie Wittman.

13

have seams at surprising spots.) These long bands are then cut into segments and made into pattern bands. Annie Jim notes that ten yards of a straight band will make about four yards of one of her favorite patterns. The design has repeating ⅜-inch (1-cm*) segments.

Segments

After your bands are made, you are ready to cut each into the preplanned segments of your pattern. Remember to include ½-inch (2-cm*) seam allowance in each segment measurement. Cuts can be either perpendicular or at an angle to the long edge; but the cuts must always be absolutely parallel to each other. One pattern may require the same band to be cut into segments of varying widths. Measure and cut precisely, grouping your cut segments in stacks, according to size.

Frances Densmore summed up the Indians' procedures in the *American Indian Hobbyist* (September/October, 1959):

The cloth is torn into strips and cut into blocks of the desired size and shape. For this, the [Seminole] women use very fine, sharp scissors with long, slender blades. The blocks are placed in little piles, each size by itself, ready to use. Thus a woman was seen with several piles of small squares and triangles near her left hand, on the edge of her sewing machine, where she could put them under the needle in the desired order without basting. The banding is made in long strips which are folded away ready to be inserted in skirts and blouses, or in dresses for little children or old men.

Fabric Work

Your work with cutting and assembling paper patterns leads easily to cutting and sewing with cloth. *When converting from paper to cloth, however, you must add seam allowance to each piece.* Allow ¼ inch (1 cm*) for each seam allowance, which adds ½ inch (2 cm*) to each torn strip and ½ inch (2 cm*) to each segment. Make outside strips, along the top and bottom of a pattern band, wider when the segments are cut on the diagonal to provide ample room for placement.

Go through the several following sample patterns, which are given in definite measurements. Once you are comfortable with these, you will find it easy to use the diagrams given in units or modules rather than inches or centimeters. Had the diagrams used inches or centimeters as units of measurement, any change from a given size would have involved minute measur-

ing or working with awkward fractions. Using the unit system makes it easy to adapt your patterns to any size you wish. Study the section "Reading the Diagrams" (page 22) and the following general directions. Then try the patterns that are most exciting for you.

For the first sewing exercises use a three-strip band; the seams of the center strip provide points for lining up your segments. Without the center-strip guide you must measure or mark each segment for accurate line-up, as explained on page 18. The patterns in *Fig. 30* are a good place to start. As you gain experience, you will do complex designs easily; to make them simply takes more time and more precision.

All of these first experiment patterns can be done with one band made up of three single strips that are only a few inches wide and that have been cut or torn the full 45-inch (114-cm) width of the fabric. Choose three colors or tones, one darker, one medium, and one light, in a cotton or cotton-blend broadcloth or similar firm weave. Make sure the fabric is torn or cut straight with the grain; adjust if necessary. Measure and tear one 2-inch (5-cm*) strip from each of the darker fabrics and one 1¼-inch (3-cm*) strip from the lightest one, selvedge to selvedge. Remember to clip through the selvedge before tearing. Lightly spray-starch and press each of the torn strips, and join along the torn edge, one of the darker strips to the lightest strip with an exact ¼-inch (1-cm*) seam. Since torn edges do not give an exact line to measure from, you may want to mark the seam line. I measure from about the midpoint of the "fringe." The Seminole women always tear, as do many of the most precise artists, but others are uncomfortable with the imprecise edge. Try it for now; you may get used to it. Remember that the tearing motion is part of the rhythm of the Seminole method. The second seam to be sewn on a strip is best measured and marked from the first line of stitching rather than from the yet-to-be-sewn edge; this ensures accuracy. The transparent grid ruler makes the marking of such parallel lines easy. After marking and sewing, press both seams flat and in the same direction. You now have a three-strip band, ready to be cut into the segments needed for these first patterns.

The ratio of the width of the segment to the width of the center strip is important to the final pattern. If the center shapes are to be square, that is, equal on all sides, then the segments must be cut the same width as the finished center strip *plus seam allowances.*

Lay your three-strip band out on a flat surface and carefully mark for ten perpendicular cuts, making each segment 1¼ inches (3 cm*) wide. Each segment is the same width as the center strip of the band was before seaming; when the segments are joined the piece in the center will be square. If you cut a segment narrower than the center strip, the result will be a

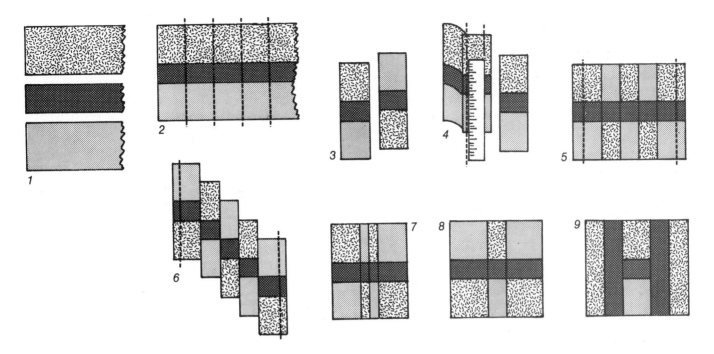

Fig. 30. *To make straight-cut patterns, tear or cut three strips (1), and join them lengthwise (2). Cut ten segments of equal size and stack them in the order in which they'll be joined (3). Mark seam lines from an adjacent parallel seam to ensure exact alignment (4). Join five segments evenly,* *with the top and bottom strips in alternate positions (5). Join five more segments by the stair-step method (6). Simple unit designs can be made from the same band (7, 8, 9). Sizes of the segments in these examples vary, and 9 shows spacer strips added to a segment.*

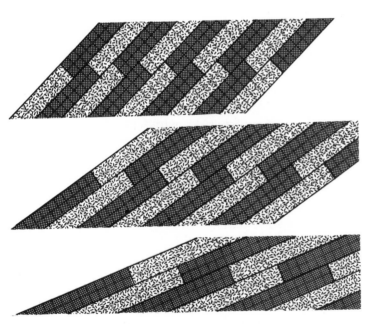

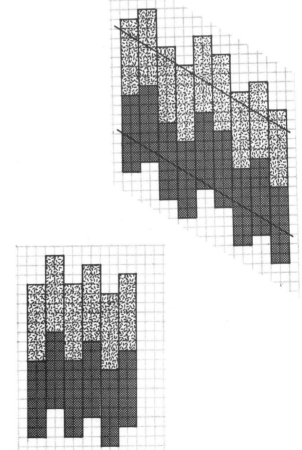

Fig. 31. *Identical segments joined at different offsets will produce different effects.*

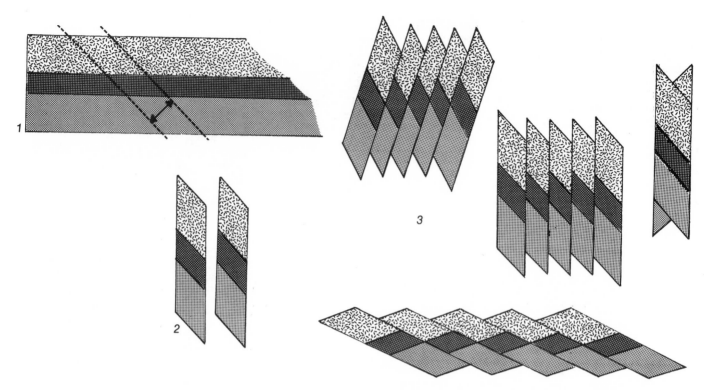

Fig. 32. *Many patterns use segments cut at an angle. These examples were cut at a 45-degree angle, but other angles can be cut also.*

1 shows how to mark the band for cutting (measurements given in this book are the distance indicated by the arrow
perpendicular to the strips). 2 shows individual segments, which can be joined in various ways, some of which are shown below. 3 shows how to line up segment points before stitching for a straight alignment.

vertically rectangular center shape; a wider segment will produce a horizontal rectangle. These shapes are useful for other patterns. Cut carefully and accurately, and stack the segments to one side.

For one pattern band, take five of these segments and stack them wrong side up, but with every other segment placed so that the darker strip is at the top. Hold or pin the first two segments together with the seams in line; stitch. Continue joining a segment at a time, always making sure that each addition is joined in the reverse direction of the one preceeding, that is, with the darkest side toward the top every other time. Put to one side.

For the next pattern band, the other five segments are joined in a stair-step fashion. Stack your remaining five segments wrong side up; this time the lighter color is always toward the top. Take the first two segments and hold with the right sides facing inward. Slide the top segment downward so that its upper seam is directly over the lower seam of the bottom segment; pin the segments together where these seams meet. Stitch together, keepng your seam a precise ¼ inch (1 cm*). Continue joining segments, each time dropping the newest segment to line up its upper seam with the lower seam of the segment before.

When doing a long band of joined segments, Lassie

finds it efficient to join them in pairs. Two segments are joined and put to one side; this is repeated until all segments are paired. Then each pair is joined to the next. Each segment or each pair can be fed under the presser foot consecutively without cutting the machine thread between pairs; they are cut apart later. This makes the work go quickly. Press your finished pattern bands, again pressing all the seams of one band in one direction.

Angle Segments

Now you are ready to try some angles. To measure the widths of angle segments, first mark one line at the desired angle of the cut, then mark succeeding lines parallel to the first line at the desired width intervals as shown in *Fig. 32* (1). Going back to the original three-strip band on the flat surface, mark a 45-degree diagonal from either of the side edges. Lay your transparent grid over that diagonal line and mark a parallel line 1¼ inches (3 cm) from it. Mark nine more parallel lines, each 1¼ inches (3 cm) apart. Cut, then put the segments into two equal stacks. You will join five of the angle segments in a straight line, but this

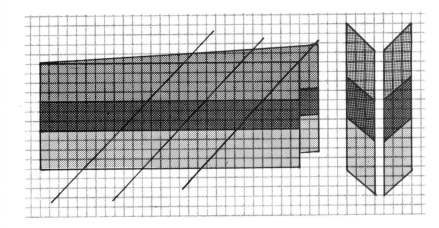

Fig. 33. *Angles of two directions can be cut at one time. Fold the band, wrong sides together, and crease. Mark the top layer of fabric only, but cut through both layers.*

Fig. 34. *Quilted spread, 104 by 128 inches (264 by 325 cm) highlighting the use of angles. By Carol Tate.*

time the seam lines do not line up and you will need to plan alignment. For this, lay two angle segments together face to face with their two upper points lined up against a straightedge and their side edges in line (*Fig. 32, 3*). Pin securely in place, and stitch a ¼-inch (1-cm*) seam along one side where both edges overlap. You might want to set your machine stitches longer on these first tries; it will make it easier to rip them out and readjust the alignment. You will soon get the hang of it. Line up the next segment, again with the two top points even, and continue the process until all five segments are joined. Put aside.

The next five angle segments will be stair-stepped. Line up the upper seam of the first segment to the lower seam of the next; pin, stitch, and go on to the next segment. When pinning for stair-step or other offset, match seams at the seam line, not at the segment edge. Press. You now have two small pattern bands, each containing five angle segments.

Segments can be cut at any angle, with 45 or 60/30 degrees the most common variations. And angle segments can be cut with the angle slanting in either of two directions. While some patterns call for repeats of only one slant, other very effective patterns balance the two slants. Slants of both directions can be cut in one operation by folding your band in half, marking one side only with cutting lines, but cutting through both layers of the band at once. You tried this technique with paper. Take care to keep the fabric layers together and in place, and make the cuts precise. You'll be pleased with the efficiency of this method.

After getting a feel for the technique, try in fabric some of the patterns you first did with paper. Whether the finished angles slant to the right or to the left is determined by the joining. In stair-step joining, segments stepped downward from left to right will slant to the left when turned horizontally. If they are stepped upward from left to right or stepped downward from right to left the slant will be to the right. Ease of working will probably be more important to you than the direction of the slant (right-handers will choose differently than left-handers), so choose to step up or down or to work from the right or from the left according to your own comfort.

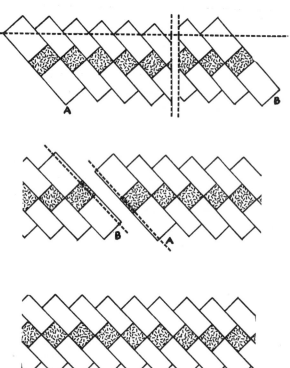

Fig. 35. To square off the angled ends of a pattern band, mark a straight line along the inner points where the segments join. Cut the band in two at a line perpendicular to your marked line and not too near either end. Join edge A to edge B. The new, squared-off ends are easier to work with.

Fig. 36. Front and back of a dress coordinating the unit design of the front with the running repeats across the back yoke. By Joanne Hill.

Angle segments can be joined straight or at an angle. The amount of shift up or down, segment to segment, is called the offset and establishes the degree of the angle and also affects the shape of the center unit of the design. Elongated diamonds placed end to end at one angle become a series of parallelograms at a different angle. The drawings show more of these relationships.

If your pattern joins other than where two seams meet or if, as with two-strip bands, the single seam cannot be used as a guide for an offset, then each segment must be marked for accurate alignment. The easiest time to do this is before all of the segments are cut. First, determine the exact offset by cutting two segments from the band. Lay them side by side, and shift them until the offset is where you like it. On one segment, mark where a cross seam of the other touches—be sure to mark at the *seam line* of the first segment, not the edge. With this first mark as a guide, you can now mark the rest of your band. Find the exact

distance between the seam and the mark on your sample. Mark at that distance, exactly parallel to that seam, the full length of the band. If you can, choose a medium- or dark-toned strip to mark so you can use a soap sliver marker. On light-colored fabric, mark the segment cut lines first. Then, with your ruler parallel to the seam line, draw a short pencil line across each cutting line, long enough to be just visible after seaming: for instance, mark across the ¼-inch (1-cm*) seam allowance with a line ⅝ inch (1.5 cm) long. This will leave a tiny mark showing when the seam is sewn—so small it is hardly noticeable, but there to guide you.

Individual segments can be marked with lines or pins after cutting, but this takes more time.

A pattern band of angle segments starts and ends with angled rather than perpendicular edges. Since most segments of pattern bands are set into other material straight, these angled ends do not fit. This problem can be solved (see *Fig. 35*). Mark a straight

Fig 37. Pattern samples. Many of the patterns in these photos and diagrams are extended from simple central pattern units by the use of surrounding strips or segments.

line along the inner points, where the segments join. Mark a line perpendicular to this line on the main band width—anywhere but on the last few segments, because if you work too close to the angle area, it is harder to be precise. Cut the band in two at the perpendicular line. Move the left angle end over the right angle end, and sew in line with the band pattern. With the angles joined, the new ends are perpendicular, and your pattern band is rectangular.

Units

You will have about ten inches (twenty-five cm) of your original three-strip band left after doing the straight and angle cut exercises, enough to make one or two simple unit designs. Unit designs differ from the running repeats of the other exercises in that they are self-contained squares or, occasionally, rectangles. When joined, these are often separated by a spacer of plain fabric. They can also be used individually as appliqué or insert. See what segment arrangements you can come up with.

The Indian women join and cut so many bands at once that they are left with few scraps. But our projects are likely to be smaller, and we usually make and cut one band at a time. This leaves triangles of fabric left

over from each end of every angle band and, if angles of two directions were cut at once, an additional triangle from the center fold. Modern artists have incorporated these triangles into their work in various ways. You can begin to explore ways to use triangles in paper play and then go on to fabric. With triangular pieces you can turn corners, jog up or down to another level within your design, lead from one area to another, or twist back to form a U shape or a box. Change the traditional technique further by adding plain areas of sewn but uncut bands, and make these long lines of color lead wherever you, the artist, wish. Then you will have one of the main keys to arranging Seminole patchwork into contemporary design.

With these exercises behind you, you are ready for Seminole patchwork.

All you need to know to construct any pattern is:
1. The number of bands used.
2. The number and sizes of strips in each band.
3. The number, width, and angle of each segment.
4. The order and angle of each join.

Our diagrams will tell you.

Fig. 38. Indian-made hot pads. Pattern in the upper left is the Broken Arrow pattern.

Patterns

This section of the book contains diagrams of patterns that range from easy to more demanding. The patterns were collected from every available source and are ones found on Seminole garments unless otherwise noted. For several years both Lassie and I have analyzed and sketched every pattern we could find. We have each, individually and several different times, visited the homes and work spaces of Indian women who were gracious enough to share and explain. We have photographed and sketched from museum collections and from private collections. We have spent hours with magnifying glasses analyzing photos of Seminole gatherings in books and magazines.

We discovered that no written record of the Seminole patterns existed. New clothes are made for tribal ceremonies, especially for the yearly Green Corn Dance in June. A Seminole woman exchanges ideas for patterns in the same way another might exchange recipes: she sees something she likes and maybe asks the maker how to do it, or maybe she tries to come up with the design on her own. Mary Frances Cypress, of the Big Cypress Reservation, spread out for us a many-yards-long sampler: one trial pattern joined to the next—121 in all. Each time she sees a pattern she likes, she makes up a sample and attaches it to her ever-growing record.

As our sketchbooks and file cards grew in number,

Lassie and I were frequently frustrated by the lack of a system in our record keeping to check whether or not we had already sketched a particular pattern. One pattern structure can have a dozen or more color arrangements, each forming an entirely different visual shape, even though the seaming is identical. No system we tried seemed to account for each variation until we hit on the one used here. That was a big step forward for this book and for anyone who wants to sew Seminole patchwork.

Follow the steps in "Reading the Diagrams" and you will be able to analyze the patterns we have diagramed, as well as any pattern you come across in your own travels or studies. You will also be able to diagram any pattern you devise yourself. Patterns will continue to develop, and Lassie and I hope to include in our file any new ones we learn about.

Traditional Patterns and Symbols

Some say Seminole patterns once held symbolic significance, others say not. Some of the early designs do have names associated with them. The world of the people who made them was sometimes recorded in abstract symbolic shapes rather than in written lan-

Fig. 39. *Band of sample patterns, collected and joined by Mary Frances Cypress, Big Cypress Reservation, Florida.*

20

Fig. 40. *Samples cut from pattern bands made by Annie Jim, Tamiami Trail. The basket made of sweet grass is typical Seminole work.*

to an association of one pattern with one woman and with her clan, which wore the clothing she made.

Even if individuals or clans cannot be positively identified by a particular pattern, the Florida Indians' designs can certainly be identified. There was an attempt several years ago to copyright eight or ten of the early patterns to protect them against non-Indian commercial use. But invention is not protected when something has been in the public domain, and the request was denied. Yard goods have been printed with Seminole patterns, and one large department-store chain used the design for sheets.

As dynamic as the designs are, however, it is the technique, the concept of construction, that was the real innovation. Fortunately for us, it wasn't patented.

1(4)SS

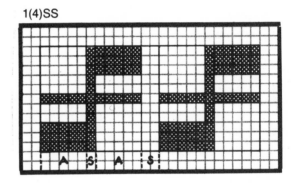

Directions for reading this diagram are on page 22.

guage. Rain, fire, and lightning were among the earliest abstractions. The Greek cross with four arms of equal length is an ancient symbol found in the pottery of southeastern Indians and in early Seminole patchwork. The arms may represent the four cardinal directions, and the cross within a circle may represent the circle of life, a symbol of major significance to the Seminole. Man-on-horseback is a pattern seen in early photographs and represents authority. There are arrow designs, a broken arrow suggesting peace.

Designs from nature are usually trees, birds, crawdads, turtles, and the small diamond shape, thought to represent the diamondback rattler, often used in the patchwork of a shaman's coat. Simple black-and-white checkerboards were made very early and are sometimes said to have been inspired by the Ralston Purina box. Colors are not used symbolically.

While a design is not owned exclusively by any one woman, she may like and use it so much that her work becomes recognized by "her" pattern. One woman I visited knew immediately who had made the skirt I had purchased the day before. Some people told me that at one time the bottom row on a skirt always indicated the woman's clan; others said not. Given this ability of the women to recognize each other's work, it is easy to believe that style habits may have led

Fig. 41. *Section of early skirt panel with traditional patterns of (top to bottom)* Fire, Trees, *and* Man-on-horseback. *From the collection of Lassie Wittman.*

Reading the Diagrams

Seminole patterns—traditional or contemporary—can be worked in any size. That is part of their appeal. Early work of the Indian women is larger in scale than what they have been doing in more recent years. As recently as the mid-1970s the patchwork typically had pieces of a width as small as ⅛ inch (.32 cm) and gave an impression of very intricate work. Today the work, especially that made to sell, is getting larger in scale again. And the scale becomes larger still in much of the work done by contemporary non-Indian artists for wall panels or quilts.

When you're adapting size, the secret is to keep all parts of a design in the same proportions to each other. To do this, Lassie and I have drawn all of the patterns to a module system on graph paper. Using this system, you can immediately read any of the diagrams and discover the number of bands involved, the number of strips in each band, and their relative measurements and placement. Let's look at *Figs. 43, 44* and *45*.

Adjacent to each pattern diagramed you will see numbers, such as 1(5) or 2(4,2). These numbers indicate, first, the number of bands and, second, the number of strips needed to make up the band or bands. The numbers also provide a way to categorize the patterns. A pattern can be quickly identified as a one-band pattern, a three-band pattern, or whatever, by the first number. Obviously, a pattern that requires only one band is quicker to make than one that takes three—or seven. The number of strips you need to tear and sew to make up each band is indicated by the numbers in parentheses just after the band number and is listed for each band in order, left to right, as it appears in the patterns. *Fig. 44* has the numbers 2(4,4) showing that two bands are needed. Band A, at the left in the design, is made up of four strips; band B, immediately to the right, also needs four strips. After the parentheses, one or more S's will sometimes appear, indicating that a spacer or insertion of plain fabric is needed in the pattern. Some patterns require spacers of more than one color or size; there will be one S for each color or size. Thus, one S means that all spacers used are cut from a single strip; S,S,S means that three spacer strips must be cut, each of a different width or color.

Under or along one side of each pattern are dotted lines separated by capital letters. The lines show where one segment is sewn to the next; the letters indicate the number and placement of segments. In *Fig. 44*, the letters are A,B,B,A. This shows that segments from two bands, A and B, have been used, each twice and in the order shown. The second B and A are in an upside down, or flipped, position.

2(4,3)

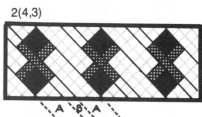

A B A

Fig. 42. James E. Billie, chairman of the Seminole Tribe and rattlesnake handler and alligator wrestler at Dania Indian Village, Hollywood, Florida. It is easy to see why the pattern in his vest is thought to represent the markings of the diamondback rattler.

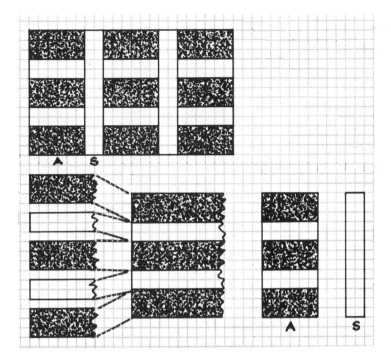

Fig. 43. *The pattern at the top has repeats of identical segments (A) separated by spacers (S). Only one band is needed for the segments, and only one strip is needed for spacers of plain fabric torn the same width as the band. This information is stated as reference number 1 (5) S: 1 band (5 strips) 1 spacer.*

Each diagram in this book can be analyzed by counting grid units to determine relative sizes of each strip, band, and segment. Here, segment A has three strips three units wide of one color, and two strips two units wide of another color. These join to form one band, which is cut in straight segments six units wide. The spacers are two units wide. Remember to add seam allowance to every tear and cut size.

Join segments alternating with spacers (an order referred to as A,S,A,S) to give you your pattern band.

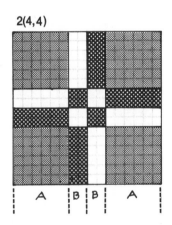

Fig. 44. *The segments are repeated evenly to make a symmetrical pattern that can be used straight or on a diagonal.*

Fig. 45. *This pattern is symmetrical as a diagonal but not as a vertical or horizontal, and is most effective only in this position.*

The pattern in *Fig. 45* uses identical colors side by side. When taking this pattern from paper to cloth, seams may be eliminated in the single color section by cutting the strip that goes into the band wide enough to span the entire space. Band A could be made of three color strips instead of five, as the grid alone suggests. Where practical, the diagramed patterns show such seams eliminated, but there may be times when you want to leave them in. Seams provide structural strength that is advisable if the expanse becomes large or the fabric is not very firm. Also, the visibility of the grid sometimes becomes a component of a design, and the pattern seems unbalanced without each line, or certain lines, in place. Seam lines can provide line-up points for joining segments, and it may take less time to sew that line-up than to mark it. Experience will soon make these decisions easy.

There are two approaches to adapting the diagramed patterns to your own size. One is to start with a total measurement and divide it into parts. The other is to start with the smallest part and add to it to get a total measurement. Either way, you count each square of the graph paper as one unit of measurement and assign your own size to that unit.

Let's take the first approach with the diagonal pattern shown in *Fig. 47*. Count the units or squares

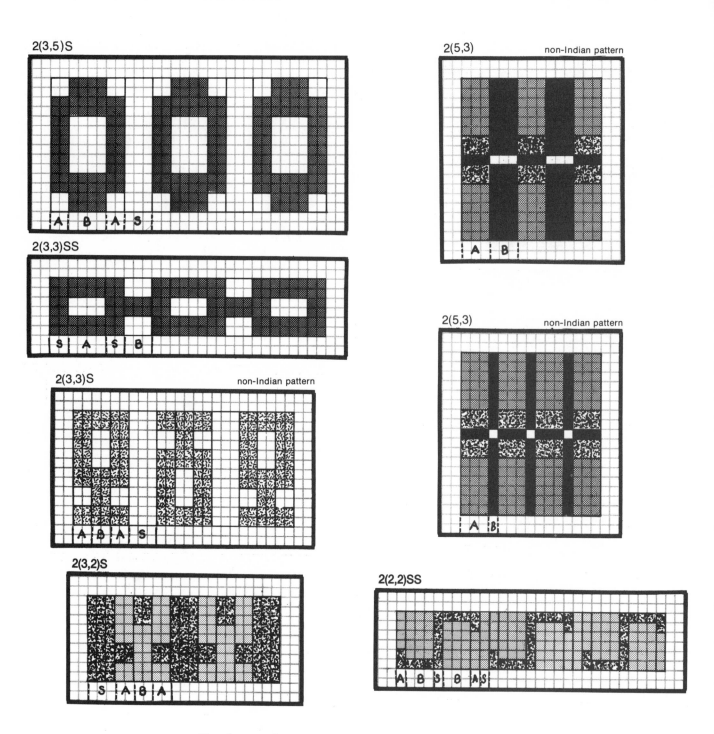

2(3,5)S

2(3,3)SS

2(3,3)S   non-Indian pattern

2(3,2)S

2(5,3)   non-Indian pattern

2(5,3)   non-Indian pattern

2(2,2)SS   non-Indian pattern

Simple repeating patterns requiring only two bands. The section, "Reading the Diagrams," explains how to use the diagrams shown here and throughout the book.

Fig. 46. *Non-Indian pattern by Jill Nordfors.*

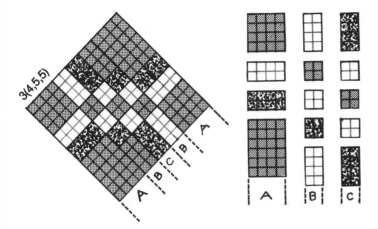

Fig. 47. Unit numbers can be adapted easily to inches or centimeters in two ways. One way is to start with a total measurement and divide it into parts. The other is to start with the smallest part and add to it in order to get a total.

This pattern is most effective when placed diagonally. The segments are marked along the right diagonal. The reference number of this pattern is 3(4,5,5), its segment arrangement is A,B,C,B,A, and its size is 14 units by 14 units.

On the right, the three segments (A,B,C), are separated to make the units of each area easy to count. The segment from the four-strip band A is cut four units wide. The band strips are four, two, two, and six units wide. Assign a measurement to each unit, add seam allowances at each edge, and you have the key to any of the diagrams in this book.

and you will find fourteen horizontal and fourteen vertical units. Suppose you want the finished pattern to be 7 inches square; each unit will equal ½ inch. If you are working in the metric system, make each pattern 14 by 14 centimeters, making each unit equal to 1 centimeter. Counting the vertical units in each segment and adding seam allowances tells you how many ½-inches (or centimeters) wide each strip must be torn. Band A must have strips 4, 2, 2, and 6 units wide, which multiply by ½ to make strips of 2, 1, 1, and 3 inches wide. (Multiplied by 1 cm, strips will be 4, 2, 2,

and 6 cm wide.) Add a ½-inch (2-cm) seam allowance to each strip, and tear-widths in band A are 2½, 1½, 1½, and 3½ inches (6, 4, 4, and 8 cm). Horizontally, band A is 4 units (2 inches, 4 cm) plus a seam allowance of ½ inch (2 cm), so you would cut 2½-inch (6-cm) segments of band A for this pattern. Band A is indicated for two segments by the letters below, the second used in a reversed, or upside-down, position. Joins line up at matching cross seams in this pattern; if they do not, I would measure and mark segments for alignment, as explained on page 18. Note that the centimeter

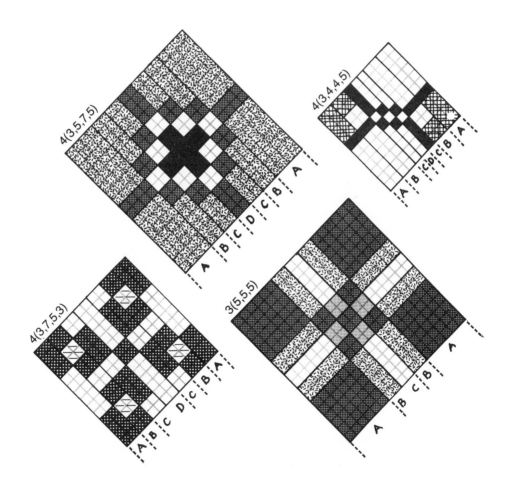

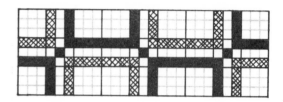

Fig. 48. *Patterns will vary in a number of ways. These patterns are identical structurally; all have three bands of five strips each 3(5,5,5). But different designs are established* *by the way one pattern meets the next and by value placement within the structure.*

measurements given here are not equivalents of inches; they are simply convenient measurements for use in the metric system.

The second approach is to count the parts to find the whole measurement. Find the smallest part in the pattern and assign to it a measurement. In this pattern the smallest elements are 2-by-2 units. If you assign a ½-inch (1 cm) measurement to each unit, the center strips of all bands are 1 inch (2 cm) wide. Band A has a top strip of 4 units (2 inches, 4 cm) and a bottom strip of 6 units (3 inches, 6 cm). Add seam allowances and you have the same final tear-width measurements as you got with the first approach.

In practice you will probably use both methods together, estimating an overall size and finding divisions within it that don't require a lot of fractions. Remember that it's easy to make changes while planning on paper. Then once your plan is set, be consistently accurate with your fabric.

Pattern Variations

As you get more involved with Seminole concepts, you'll begin to notice the factors that create change. One pattern may look entirely different from another yet be identical to it in construction. As you plan your own patterns and figure out how to join them, consider the following.

The variable characteristics of any pattern include:
The number of bands used.
The width of each strip.
The width of each cut segment.
The insertion of spacer strips within the pattern.
The angle of cutting the segments.
The angle of joining the segments.
The reversal of some segments.
The sequence of joining segments. (Two bands joined A,B,B,A will differ from the same bands joined A,B,A,B.)

The arrangement of completed units can be varied by:
Varying the angles at which segments are joined or inserted. Segments can be perpendicular to the base line or at any angle to it.
Reversing alternating pattern units.
Alternating two or more design units.
Adding surrounding strips to extend the pattern.
Cutting a pattern band in half lengthwise; for instance, making two bands of triangles out of one band of diamonds.

Add to these lists the many color possibilities for each strip, spacer, or surround, and you will see that variations are almost limitless.

PATTERN DIAGRAMS

This section is almost exclusively pattern diagrams. Each pattern can be made in any size and in numerous combinations of color. Directions and suggestions for methods of joining and inserting patterns have been given already. Each pattern has a reference number, telling you the number of bands and strips needed to make it. The sequence in which the segments are joined is always left to right. Find the patterns that interest you, and use them in your own specially designed projects.

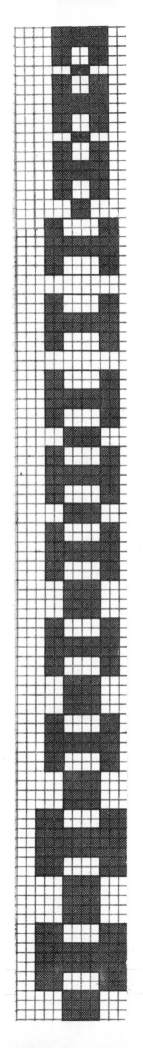

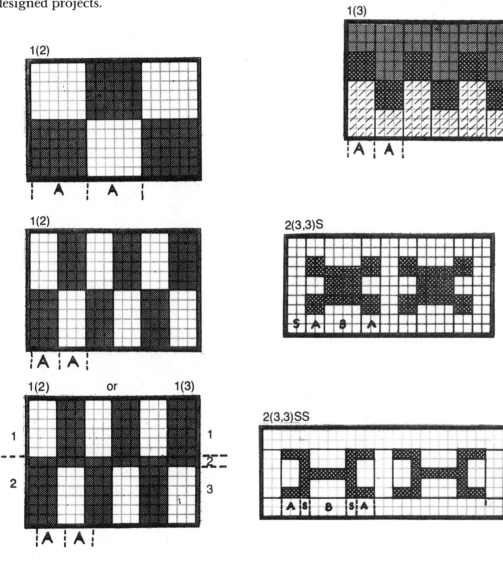

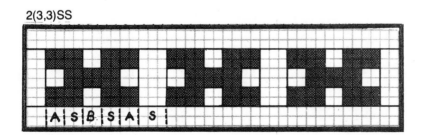

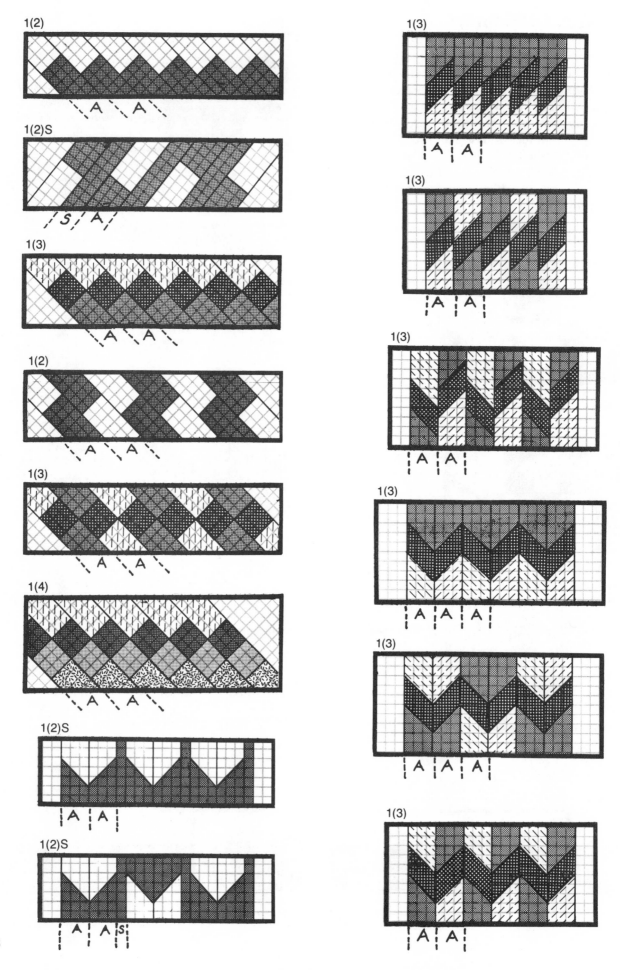

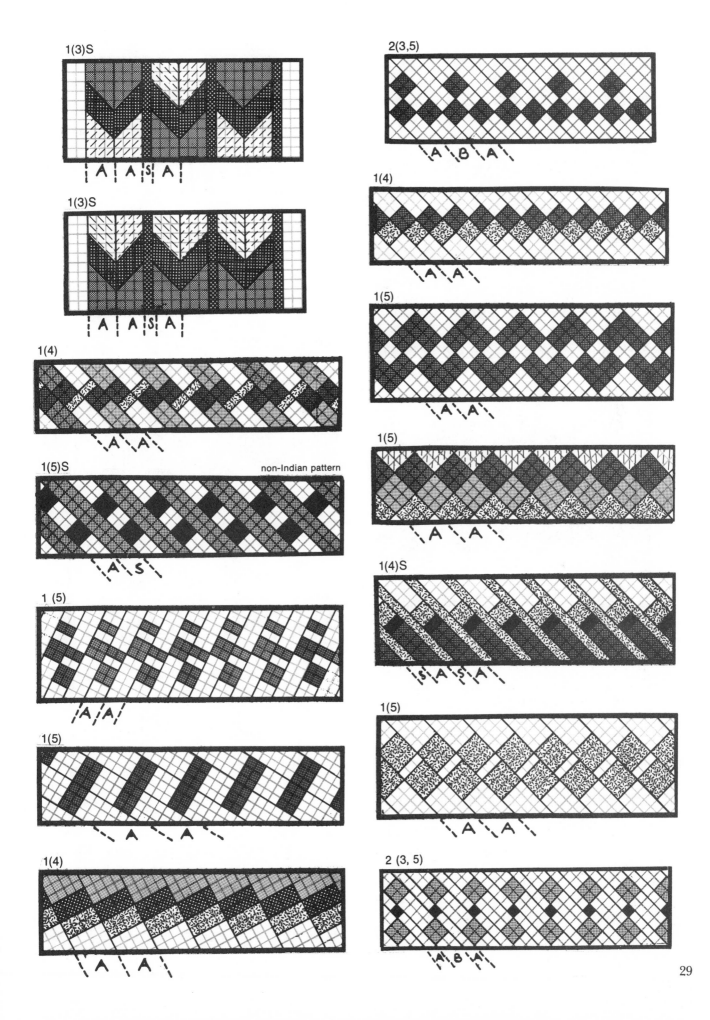

1(3)S

1(3)S

1(4)

1(5)S   non-Indian pattern

1 (5)

1(5)

1(4)

2(3,5)

1(4)

1(5)

1(5)

1(4)S

1(5)

2 (3, 5)

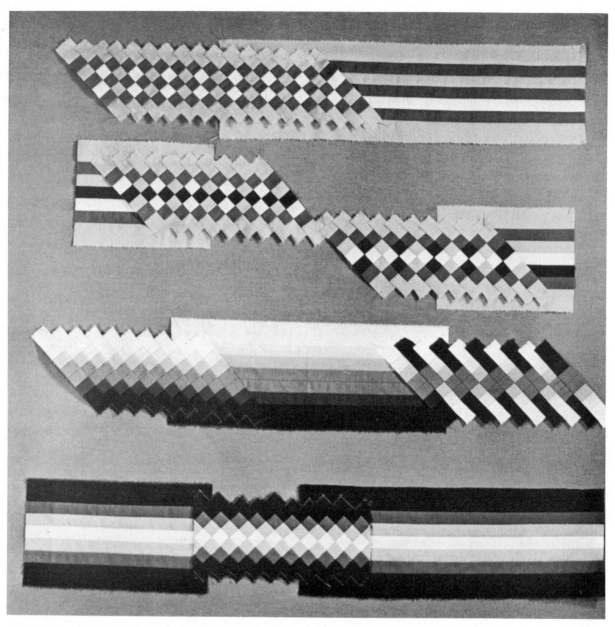

Fig. 49. *Checkerboard patterns by Lassie Wittman. Segments are cut equal to the torn strips, making each "mosaic" identical and square. Lassie tears the outside strips of each band wider, which allows her to vary the trim width. (Second row from the bottom) Two patterns made from one band: one pattern has all of the segments right side up; the second has alternate segments upside down.*

Checkerboards

Some of the most versatile constructions fall in what I call the checkerboard series. These patterns characteristically fit the identical square spaces of a grid and can be worked out easily on graph paper.

The construction of each pattern is the same, but the number of strips and bands used varies. Strips are all of equal width, and segments are all cut the same width as the tear-width of the strips. The segments are then joined in the order called for. Precision is necessary to make the units line up—the space between seam lines, both horizontal and vertical, must be equal, and cross seams must be matched precisely when joining. For greater accuracy, mark each seam line from its adjacent seam line, rather than from the edge.

The simple nine-patch was one of the earliest patterns, used by the colonists as well as the Seminoles. Such patterns can become quite sophisticated through color and value placement. Large squares can seem to overlap other squares, or patterns within patterns can be created.

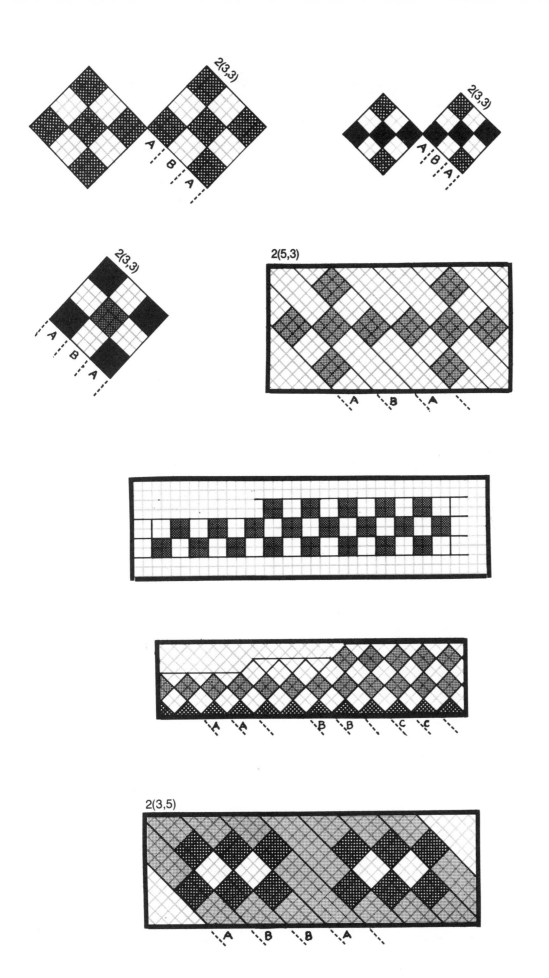

2(3,3)

2(3,3)

2(3,3)

2(5,3)

A   B   A

A   A   B   B   C   C

2(3,5)

A   B   B   A

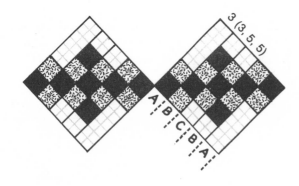

3 (3, 5, 5)

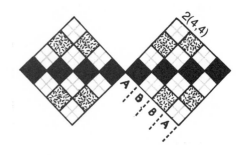

2 (4, 4)

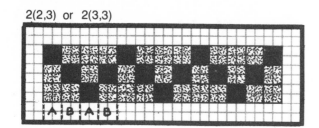

2(2,3) or 2(3,3)

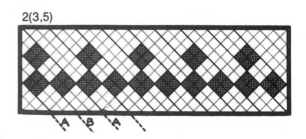

2(3,5)

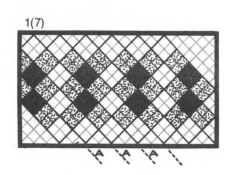

1(7)

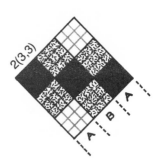

2(3,3)

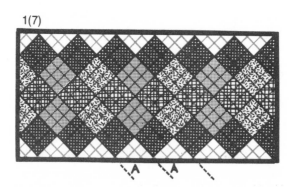

1(7)

Recognizing Angles of Segments

Some patterns are made from segments that have been cut from the band at an angle. The outside edges, top and bottom, of each segment are parallel to the cross seam, as shown in *Fig. 50*. The original bands used and angle of cut can readily be recognized even from trimmed bands.

Your drawn lines establish the original segment shape without seam allowances. The acute angle between the side edge and the bottom, or base line, is the angle at which the segment is cut.

1(3)

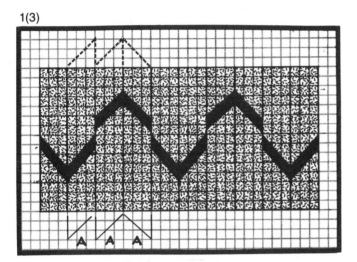

Fig. 50.

Patterns are shown here in their trimmed state; this is the way they will look when finished. If the untrimmed segment ends had been shown, in many cases it would have been difficult to recognize the patterns themselves. Segment shapes are indicated where it seemed helpful.

The pattern in *Fig. 50* has been cut from one band, with angles going in two directions. The "center" strip is not at the exact center, which creates the offset when alternate pairs of segments are joined in the reverse position.

1(5)

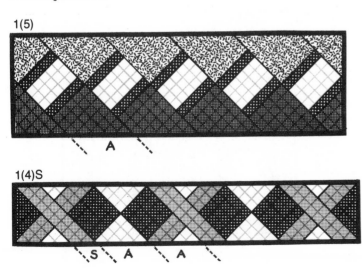

1(4)S

1(5)

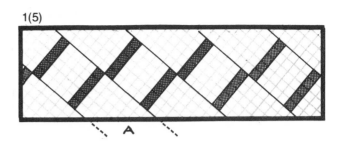

1(5)

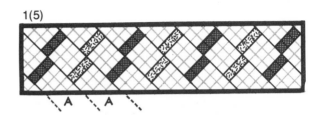

1(4)

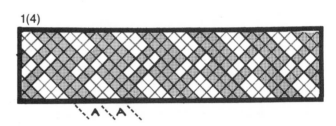

2(4,4)

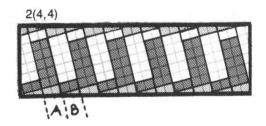

2(3,5)

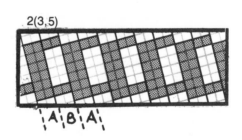

S or 2(2,3)S   non-Indian pattern

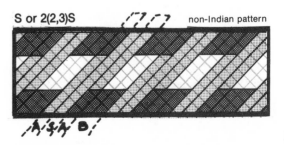

33

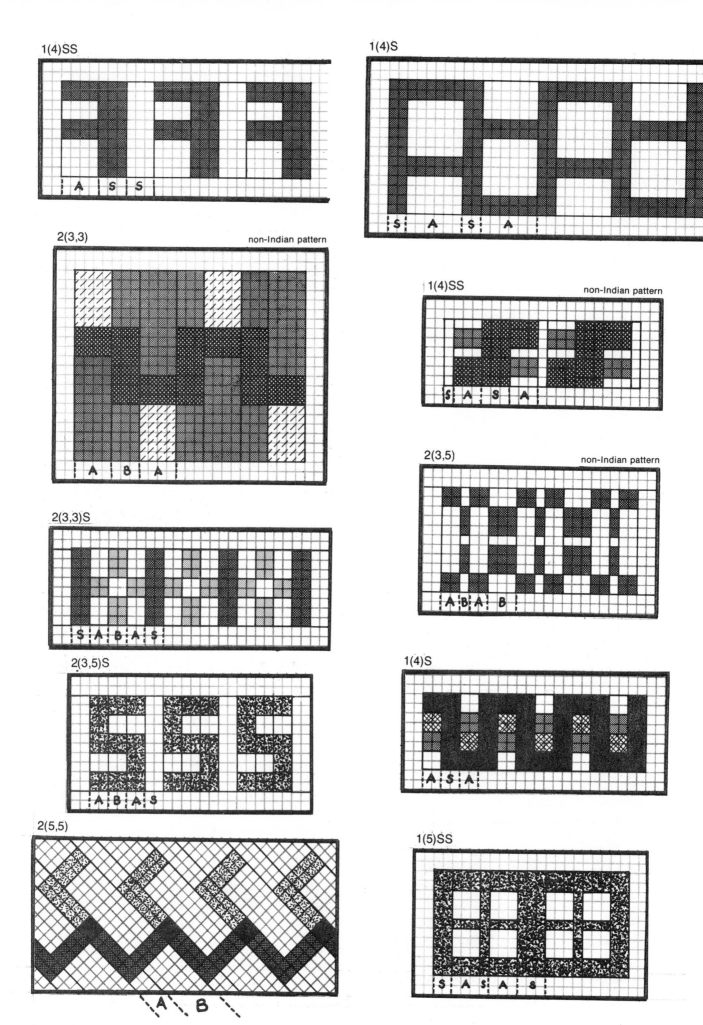

1(4)SS

A S S

1(4)S

S A S A

2(3,3)

non-Indian pattern

A B A

1(4)SS

non-Indian pattern

S A S A

2(3,5)

non-Indian pattern

2(3,3)S

S A B A S

A B A B

2(3,5)S

A B A S

1(4)S

A S A

2(5,5)

A B

1(5)SS

S A S A S

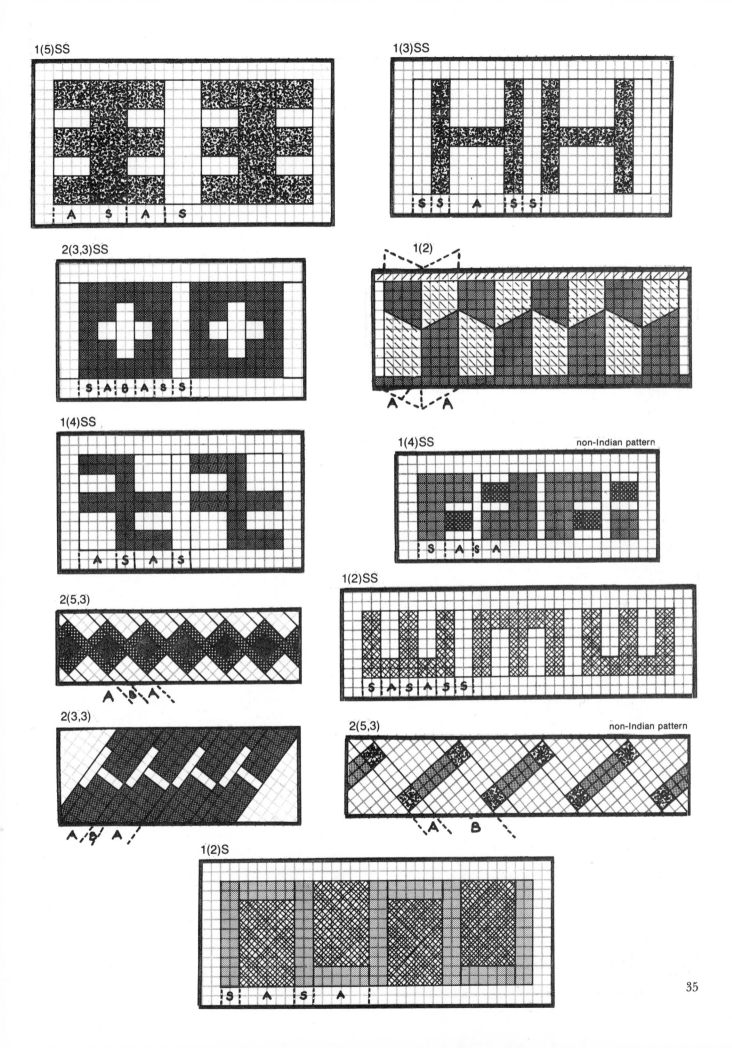

1(5)SS

1(3)SS

2(3,3)SS

1(2)

1(4)SS

1(4)SS   non-Indian pattern

2(5,3)

1(2)SS

2(3,3)

2(5,3)   non-Indian pattern

1(2)S

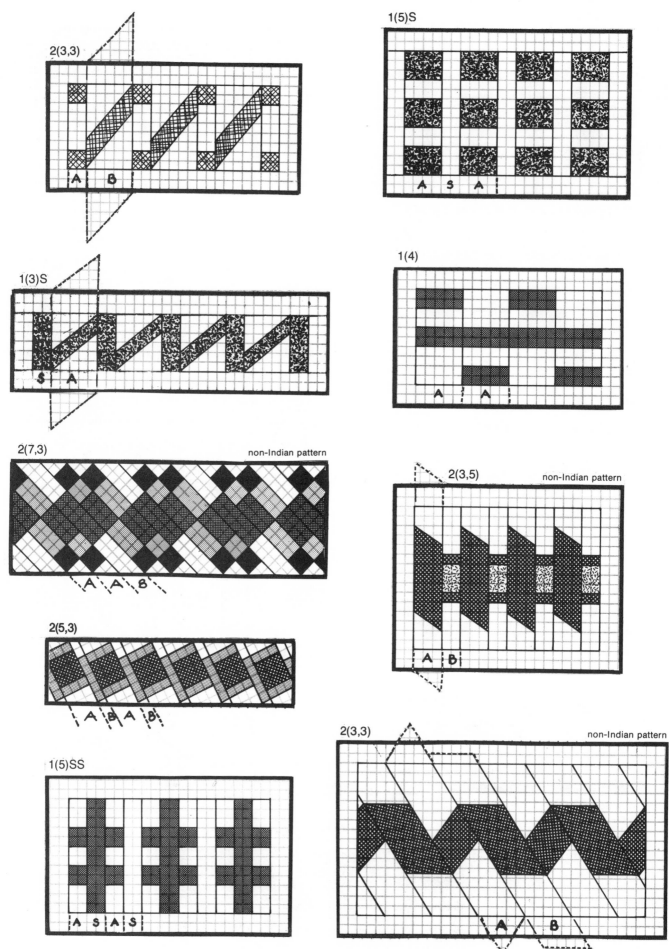

2(3,3)

1(5)S

1(3)S

1(4)

2(7,3)   non-Indian pattern

2(3,5)   non-Indian pattern

2(5,3)

1(5)SS

2(3,3)   non-Indian pattern

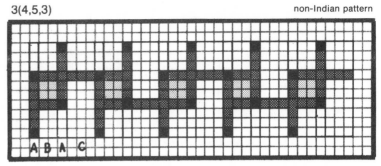

3(4,5,3)   non-Indian pattern

A B A C

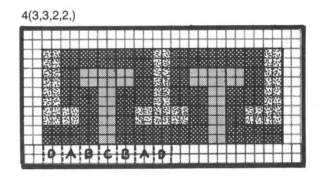

4(3,3,2,2,)

C A B C B A D

Fig. 51. *Vest with original pattern by Rosemary King.*

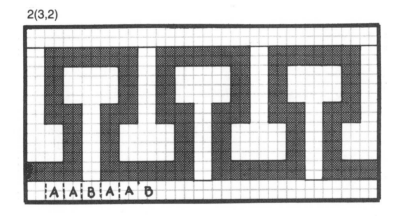

2(3,2)

A A B A A B

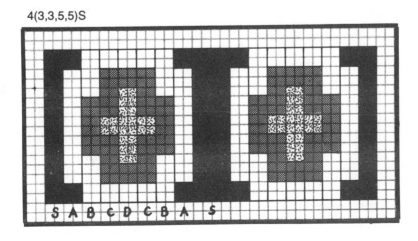

4(3,3,5,5)S

S A B C D C B A S

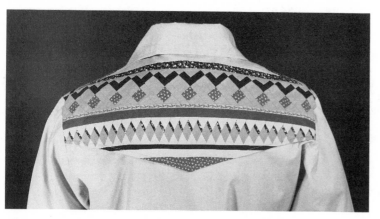

Fig. 52. *Patterns that are different but similar and have been seen on Indian garments. One pattern was used as shirt trim by Cheri Burt.*

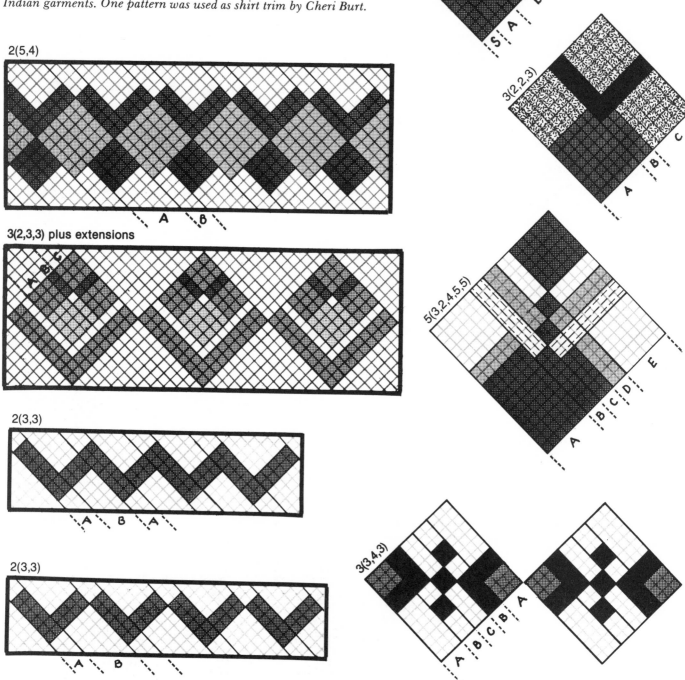

2(5,4)

3(2,3,3) plus extensions

2(3,3)

2(3,3)

4(2,3,3,3)

2(2,3)S

3(2,2,3)

5(3,2,4,5,5)

3(3,4,3)

Similar Yet Different

Part of the fascination of Seminole patchwork is the many ways that one construction can be varied to create different patterns. It is also true, however, that two patterns that appear the same may have been constructed differently. Another two patterns may be the same to a point, but one will have extra color or shape added.

Here are patterns related either by structure or design; the differences are noted in the reference numbers. Some constructions will be quicker to sew but will take more fabric than their alternates.

The two non-Indian bands in *Figs. 53* and *54* join segments at their short ends, rather than side by side as in most patterns. Of these two, the one in *Fig. 53* is made from one band of two strips of equal width. Segments are straight and equal in width to the tear width of one strip. Turn each segment 90 degrees and join one to the next to make a long band of alternating light and dark. The pattern in *Fig. 54* is made of two bands. Band A (right) is used in both patterns. Band B is made of two strips of equal width. This band is cut into angle segments also joined end to end. Join band A to band B, matching seams. Spatial illusions can be created with value contrasts.

2(4,4)

2(3,5)

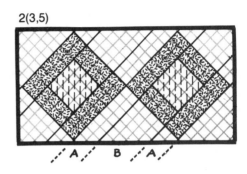

2(3,4)

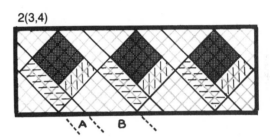

3(3,3,2) (plus extensions)

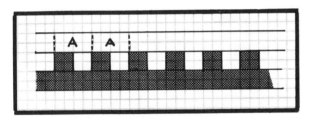

Fig. 53. *Non-Indian pattern.*

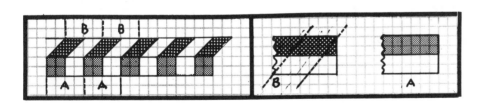

Fig. 54. *Non-Indian pattern.*

3(2,3,3) plus extensions

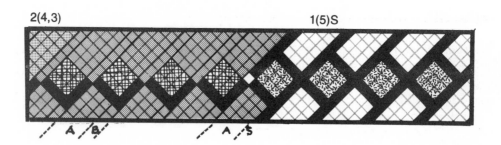

2(4,3) 1(5)S

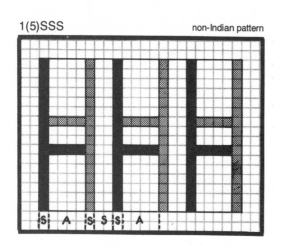

1(5)SSS non-Indian pattern

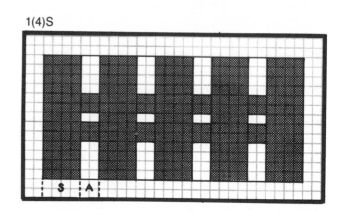

1(4)S

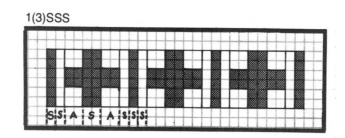

1(3)SSS

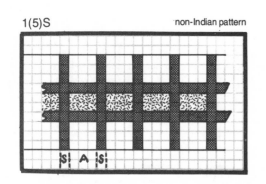

1(5)S non-Indian pattern

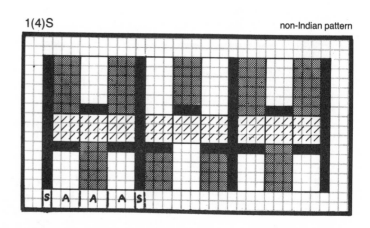

1(4)S non-Indian pattern

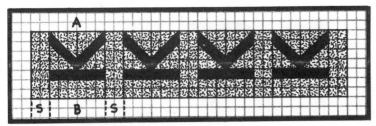

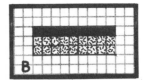

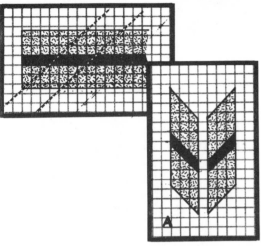

Fig. 55. *The* Bird *pattern is made of two bands. Make bands A and B, as shown in the diagrams. Fold and double-cut band A to give you equal numbers of segments with angles going in opposite directions. Join these band A segments in pairs to make slanting angles, and press. Measure the finished width of the pairs, and cut band B in segments equal to that width. Sew one band B segment straight across the angled end of one pair, just below, touching the tip of the point. Press. Repeat to make all of the pattern units needed, then join them, alternating with spacers of the background fabric.*

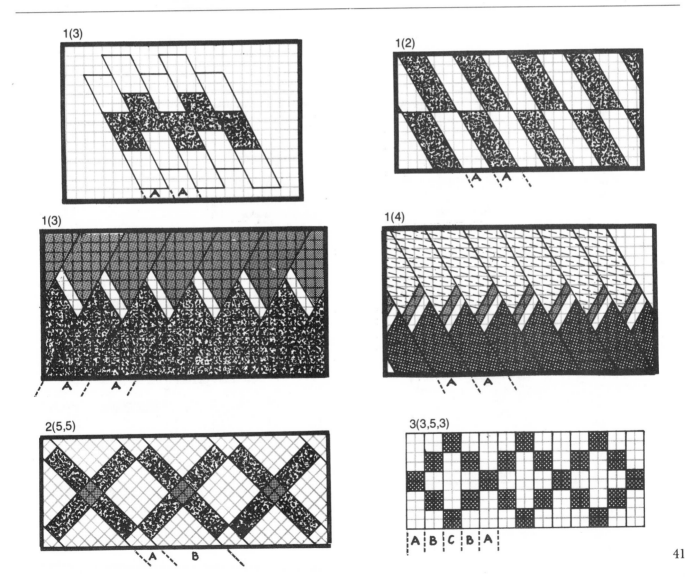

2(3,5)

A B

2(4,4)

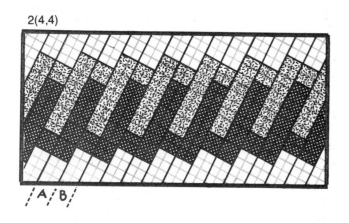

A B

3(2,5,3)S

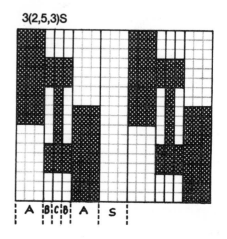

A B C B A S

2(3,4)SS

A B S B A S

3(2,3,5)

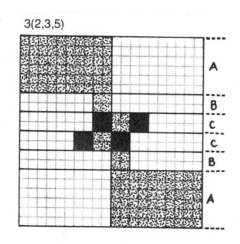

A
B
C
C
B
A

7(2,4,3,7,3,4,2)

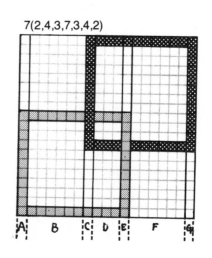

A B C D E F G

Pattern units are self-contained motifs. They may be used singly or may be joined to form a pattern band. Segments joined without a break between motifs are called running repeats. The band uses identical segments in different arrangements including a running repeat and a series of single motifs.

The differences between many of the patterns are slight, indeed almost negligible, when the patterns are seen as single units or in the limitations of black and white diagrams. But it is these slight differences that give the technique so much vitality, because the most minor change can begin a new rhythm when done in repetition.

Many of the motifs can be used equally well in an upright or diagonal position; others are only really effective in one position. Rotate the pages as you look at the patterns to see each pattern in both positions.

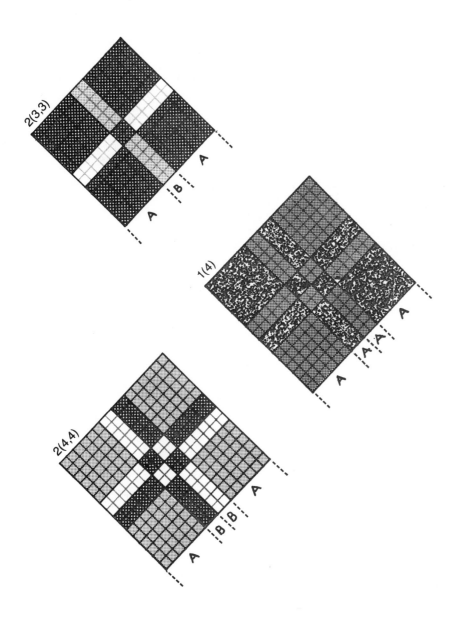

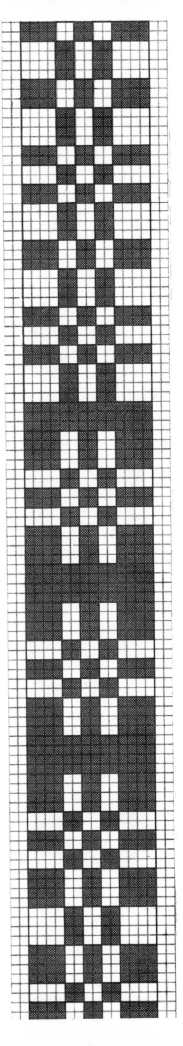

3(4,4,5)

3(3,2,3)

3(3,5,3)

3(3,5,3)

3(3,5,3) or 3(5,5,5)

3(2,3,2)

3(5,3,5) or 3(5,5,5)

3(3,4,5)

3(3,4,5) or 3(3,5,5)

3(2,3,2)

4(4,5,5,4)

3(2,5,5)

4(7,5,5,3)

5(3,7,4,5,3)

3(5,4,3)

3(3,4,3)

3(4,5,5)

3(4,5,5)

2(3,3)

3(4,4,5)

3(3,4,5)

3(5,3,5)

2(3,3)

45

2(2,3)

A : B : A

2(3,3)

A : B : B : A

2(4,4)

A : B : B : A

2(4,4)

A : B : B : A

2(3,4)

A : B : B : A

2(2,4)

A : B : B : A

2(4,4)

A : B : B : A

2(3,4)

A : B : B : A

2(4,4)   or   2(4,2)

A : B : B : A

2(3,3) or 1(3)S

A : B : A

3(3,5,3) or 3(3,5,5)

A : B : C : B : A

3(3,5,5) or 3(3,5,3)

A : B : C : B : A

47

3(5,5,5)

A ⋮B⋮ C ⋮B⋮ A

2(4,4)S

A ⋮B⋮ C ⋮B⋮ A

3(2,4,5)

A B C⋮B⋮ A

3(5,5,3) or 3(5,5,5)

A ⋮B⋮ C ⋮B⋮ A

4(4,5,5,4)

A ⋮B⋮C⋮B⋮ D

3(5,5,5)

A ⋮B⋮ C ⋮B⋮ A

3(3,4,5)

A ⋮B⋮ C ⋮B⋮ A

3(3,5,3)

A ⋮B⋮C⋮B⋮ A

3(5,5,5)

A ⋮B⋮ C ⋮B⋮ A

2(2,4)

A ⋮B⋮B⋮ A

3(3,5,5)

A ⋮B⋮ C ⋮B⋮ A

3(3,5,5)

A ⋮B⋮ C ⋮B⋮ A

49

3(5,5,5) A | B | C | B | A

3(5,3,5) A | B | C | B | A

2(3,4) A | B | B | A

3(5,5,5) A | B | C | B | A

or 3(5,5,3) A | B | C | B | A

3(5,5,5) A | B | C | B | A

3(5,5,5) A | B | C | B | D

or 3(5,5,5) 3(5,5,3) A | B | C | B | A

4(2,4,6,7) A | B | C | D | C | B | A

3(5,5,5) A | B | C | B | A

3(4,3,5) A | B | C | B | A

Figuring out how some finished patterns have been put together is difficult, but the job becomes easy enough when you know how the segments were rotated or shifted. The two *Arrow* patterns shown in *Figs. 56* and *59* are examples.

Fig. 57 is the cutting diagram for the first *Arrow* motif. The angle segments need to be equal in width to the band (although a bit more width makes things easier when sewing). Do not fold the band to double-cut this pattern; measure and cut each line precisely. Lay out the four cut segments according to *Fig. 58*. The guide letters on the band indicate how the segments have been turned.

Join the two right-side segments; join the two left-side segments. Then join the entire right side to the left side, matching the seam lines of the point. The finished pattern will look like the middle diagram. Trim the upper points and join with spacers to make the pattern band below.

Indian women sometimes make an *Arrow* pattern in two colors, the right shaft and tip in one color, the left in another. Segments are cut from two bands for this: the left shaft and right tip from one band, the right shaft and left tip from the other.

The second *Arrow* pattern (*Fig. 59*) takes three successive bands; band B is made from band A. Make band A with three strips and cut it into segments equal in width to the tear-width of the center strip. Join the

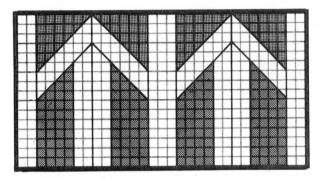

Fig. 56. Arrow *motif.*

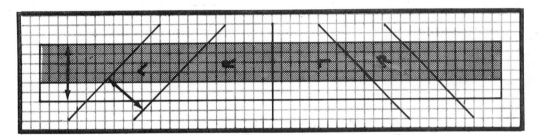

Fig. 57. *Cutting diagram for* Arrow *motif.*

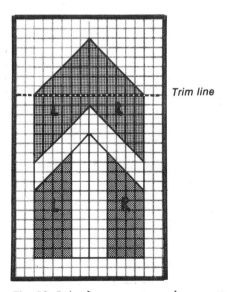

Trim line

Fig. 58. *Join the segments as shown.*

51

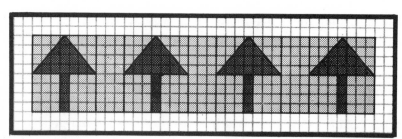

Fig. 59. Arrow *motif.*

Band B

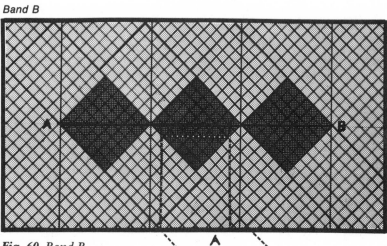

Fig. 60. *Band B.*

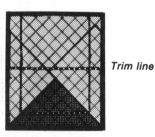

Trim line

Fig. 61. *Band-B segment.*

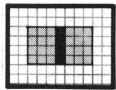

Fig. 62. *Band-C segment.*

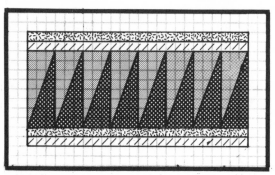

Fig. 63.

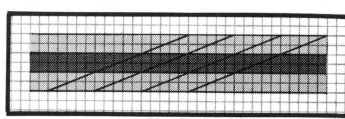

Fig. 64.

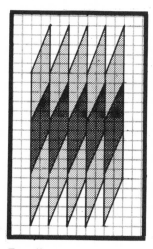

Fig. 65.

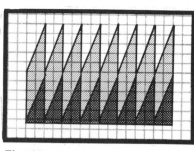

Fig. 66.

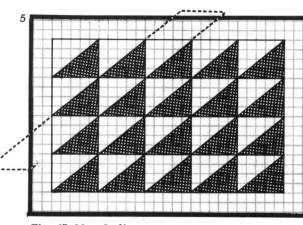

Fig. 67. *Non-Indian pattern.*

segments at 45-degree angles so that the points of the center squares touch. Press. This is band B (*Fig. 60*). When this band is cut in two horizontally, the squares become triangles and are used for arrowheads. Mark a horizontal line through the row of touching tips (a to b). Next, intersect the horizontal line with perpendicular lines marked through the touching tips. Cut along each marked line. The pieces are band-B segments (*Fig. 61*).

Band C forms the arrow shafts. Join three strips, making the center strip the width of the arrowhead-base seam line (*Fig. 62*). Cut band C into segments and join each shaft to a triangular top. Press and trim. Alternate each arrow with a background spacer to make your pattern band.

The pattern in *Fig. 63* is called *Fire* by the Indians and, with its elongated triangles spiked in a row, is dynamic and versatile. You will see it on several of the samplers pictured in this book.

The pattern can be constructed in several ways. I consider using a three-strip band to be the most efficient, but it can also be made with two bands and in various proportions and angles. The placement of torn and cut edges in some Indian work indicates that they, too, construct this pattern in more ways than one. Sometimes they piece one diagonal at a time rather than piecing by the strip method; it takes less fabric but more time.

Fig. 64 shows a three-strip band (each strip is two units wide); the segments are cut diagonally at parallel

Fig. 68. *Skirt from Kip and Krista's, Miami.*

Fig. 69.

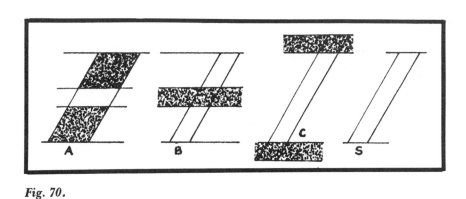

Fig. 70.

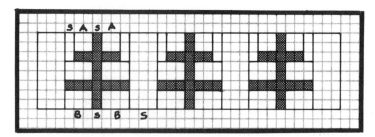

Fig. 71. Trees.

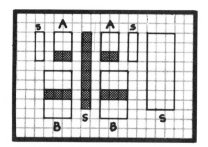

Fig. 72.

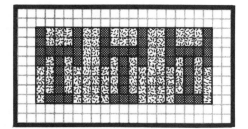

Fig. 73. Crawdad.

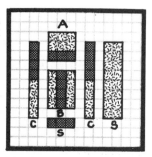

Fig. 74.

lines two units apart (plus seam allowance). When joined, the segments from this three-strip band become a pattern band and will look like *Fig. 65*. Note that this offset of segments provides for seam allowance. Cut this pattern band in half horizontally. This gives you two lengths of the pattern band, which can be joined end to end for a longer band (*Fig. 66*).

Varying the proportions will vary the pattern. The band for the center pattern of *Fig. 63* has three eight-unit strips, and the joined segments are three units wide. The non-Indian variation (*Fig. 67*) uses three four-unit strips, and the joined segments are once again three units wide. This pattern was made by joining rows of triangles along their trimmed edges, top and bottom, lining up the points precisely.

Two-strip construction requires essentially the same procedure as three-strip construction. However, the center strip of a three-strip band produces a diamond that can be cut to make two rows of triangles, while triangles are made one row at a time with a two-strip band.

The unusual skirt by Irene Cypress shown in *Fig. 68* (page 53) is nine feet around and uses about one hundred yards of rickrack. The skirt was constructed as if it were square, but the segments were cut at an angle of 60 degrees rather than 90 degrees. Segments A, B, A were joined first—cross seams matched precisely— for the center diamond (*Fig. 69*). Spacers were added at opposite sides, and then C segments were joined. Care and precision were needed in cutting the angles and in aligning the stretchy bias segments, but the effect is worth the effort. *Fig. 70* indicates the bands and the angles used to make this pattern.

The patterns for *Trees* (*Fig. 71*) and *Crawdad* (*Fig. 73*) both combine segments from several bands as construction blocks.

For *Trees,* first join the two strips for band A. Cut all of the segments you need for the number of patterns you wish to make. Add a spacer to each of these segments—on half of the segments, join the spacers to the right sides; on the other half, join to the left sides. Press and set aside.

Two of the three strips of band B are identical to band A, so band B can be made by adding another strip of any leftover band A or, if there are no leftovers, by joining the necessary three strips. Cut band B into segments equal in width to the segments from band A plus the spacer. Join a band-B segment to each band-A segment plus the spacer. Press.

Arrange your newly joined sections into right and left stacks. Join the sections, starting with a left section, adding a spacer as a tree trunk, putting in a right section, and adding a background spacer in that order. Repeat for each tree (*Fig. 72*).

Crawdad takes three bands. Band A is two strips, band B is three strips (segments from it are turned to form the vertical body section), and band C is two strips. Cut each band into its segments. Join segment A to one end of the vertical segment B, with a spacer across the other end. This grouping forms a center section. Now join one band-C segment, one center section, and a second band-C segment to make each crawdad (*Fig. 74*).

54

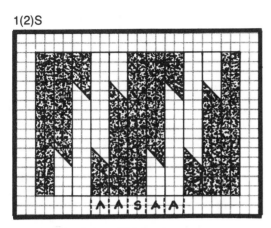

Fig. 75. *Traditional* Lightning *pattern.*

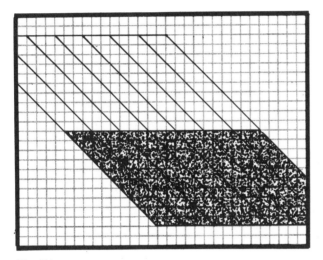

Fig. 76.

Fig. 77. Lightning *variation.*

Lightning, as shown in *Fig. 75,* is an early Indian pattern. The variation shown in *Fig. 77* was devised by Flo Wilson Campbell for her panel *Rain Cloud.*

The traditional *Lightning* is made entirely of equal segments cut from one band only, plus optional spacers. Cut the strips wide enough to make the original band one-fourth to one-third wider than the finished pattern band is to be (*Fig. 76*). This provides extra material so that the segments can be shifted up or down during joining. The first two segments are joined with the colors in the same position but the angles offset. Make as many identical pairs as you will need for the length of your pattern band. Join each pair to the next, placing every other pair upside down. Lining up the segments for this pattern is tricky but can be mastered, and the effect is worth the trouble.

Spacers may be added; the top figure shows a spacer of the darker color inserted, which makes a slight separation between each zigzag. If you use equal-sized zigzags without spacers, you can create a strong positive-negative interplay that is very dynamic.

Flo's version of *Lightning* (*Fig. 77*) is made from one three-strip band that has a narrow center strip and two outside strips, each outside strip wide enough to allow shifting. The band is cut into 45-degree angle segments of both directions and of differing widths. Do not fold the band and double-cut; single cuts give you the most flexibility. Join segment to segment, always matching the center strip precisely, but varying the order of the widths.

Special effects by Flo Wilson Campbell.

Fig. 78. Receding Image *seems three-dimensional because the segments, cut from a thirteen-strip band, are tapered: segments are 1 inch wide at the top and 1¾ inches wide at the bottom (2.5 and 4.4 cm). Black horizontal strips are part of the thirteen-strip band and seem to intersect the black vertical spacers inserted between segments.*

Fig. 79. *The in-and-out pattern—part of* Window Pane—*is made of two five-strip bands. The outer strips of both bands are identical. One band's strips are all light values; the other band's center strips are the same colors as those of the first band, but the values are darker. Segments of opposite angles alternate with each other and are separated by green spacers. The effect is one of movement.*

Fig. 80. *The light-glow pattern used in* Rain Cloud *is made from one eight-strip band; the strips are closely related in tone value, light to dark. The band was folded and six cuts were made at 45-degree angles, so there are twelve segments of two directions. Two identical pattern bands were made, each of six segments of alternating angles. Both bands were trimmed and joined along the light side of the trimmed edge.*

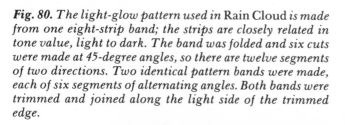

Fig. 81. *Flo Wilson Campbell's method for the isosceles triangles in* Rain Cloud, *shown in the diagram, involves straight-cut rather than angle-cut segments. Because she wanted to vary her color combinations—browns to off-whites—she made seven short, two-strip bands—each strip four units wide. Each joined segment is three units wide, and segments are also offset three units, making all sides of the triangles equal.*

Flo provided color unity by making the upper strip of every band beige Kettle Cloth; then she used different colors for each lower strip. Bands were cut into equal segments; the segments were laid out, mixed, and shifted for a random placement of colors among the lower portion, but the beige was always at the top. The segments were joined stair-stepped, and the upper and lower points were trimmed away. These pattern bands of triangles were joined, row after row, along the trimmed edges, always with the beige triangles pointing downward.

Band A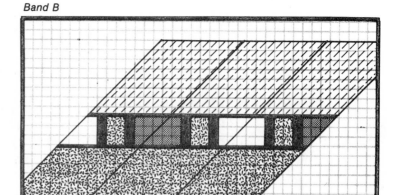

Band B

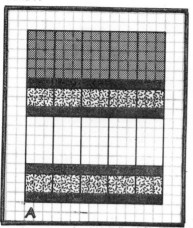

Fig. 82.

For the pattern illustrated in *Fig. 82,* narrow segments cut from band A are joined horizontally to form the center strip of band B. Band A has eight strips; band B has five strips—two wide outside strips and two narrow strips edging the center strip made from band A. Segments from band B are cut at 45-degree angles and are joined perpendicularly. The skirt in *Fig. 83* shows this pattern made in slightly different proportions.

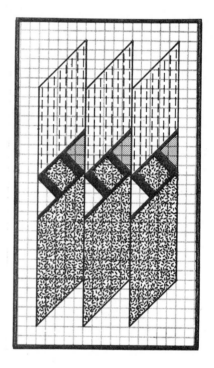

Fig. 83.

The *Broken Arrow* pattern, a traditional symbol for peace, requires three successive bands. First make band A of three strips and cut it into segments (*Fig. 84*). Join these segments alternately with wide spacers to make band B (*Fig. 85*). For band C (*Fig. 86*), sew one wide strip along the top and another wide strip along the bottom of band B. Mark 45-degree diagonals along band C, and cut it into segments. The seam lines dissect the corners of the spacers that were part of band B, so make the diagonal cut a seam-allowance width to the inside of each corner. Rotate each segment 90 degrees so that the center bars are vertical, and join the segments to form the pattern band.

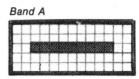

Band A

Fig. 84. *Band A.*

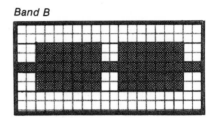

Band B

Fig. 85. *Band B.*

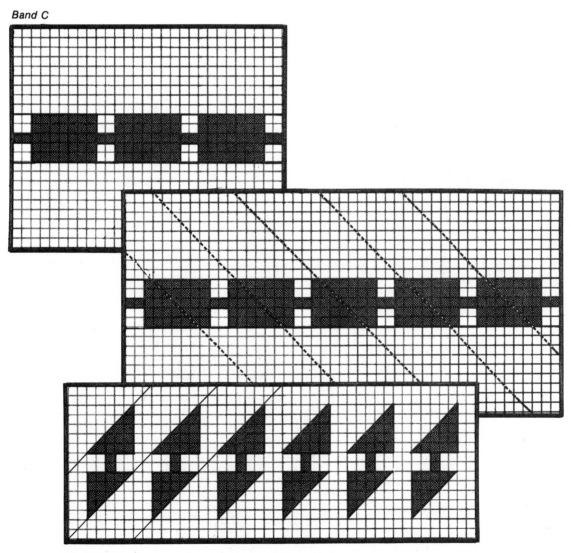

Band C

Fig. 86. *Band C.*

Fig. 87. *Vest made to match the shirt in* Fig. 52. *The courthouse-steps method was used to surround the central unit design. By Cheri Burt.*

Pattern units can be used as the first step to more complex patterns. By adding extensions of fabric you can make a unit a part of a larger segment; by surrounding a unit with strips of fabric, you can make it part of a larger unit.

The two most common methods of adding surrounding strips are the traditional *log-cabin* technique (*Fig. 89*) and a variation of it called *courthouse steps* (*Fig. 90.*) Non-Indians usually use plain strips of fabric around a single center piece to make these patterns. But Indian women see every strip added as another place to add pattern, and they add strips cut from bands that are made to match and extend their pieced centers.

Extensions can be added to any pattern unit, making it easy to assemble the resulting segments into a pattern band. To add extensions efficiently, tear two long strips, each wide enough to provide the needed extension (see *Fig. 91*); allow extra width if the segments are to be joined at an angle. Place one extension on your machine, ready to be seamed along one side. Place one unit face down on the extension, lining up the edges to be stitched. Sew in place, stopping just before the end of the unit. Lay the second unit next to the first, the two units barely touching (the space between units in drawing B is for clarity), and continue to stitch. Continue adding one unit at a time until all are stitched in place. Then cut straight across the extension at each spot where the units meet; you now have a series of units with one extension each. Repeat the process with the second extension strip, this time stitching the opposite edge of your units. When cut apart, these final pieces are full segments. (C shows one segment turned vertically.)

The pattern band in *Fig. 92* is an example of a band of segments made of units and extensions.

Diagrams of complex patterns are more useful as guides to relative sizes and proportions than as definitive sewing guides because usually there is more than one construction possible for any one pattern. A Greek cross is diagramed (*Figs. 96–98*) both as joined segments and as a center unit design surrounded by strips added in the log-cabin method. The first takes several more steps to create than the second. But I have seen it done both ways.

The first step in planning a complex pattern is to determine the central unit; that is the part that you will sew up in segments. This unit can also be constructed in several ways. *Fig. 93* demonstrates the way I would make that particular pattern, but it can also be made entirely of log-cabin strips (*Fig. 89*) surrounding the single-piece center square. Or, for the first surround I can add two spacer strips across the opposite sides, then add two C segments in courthouse-steps fashion. Often, no one construction is better than another.

Fig. 88. *Pattern band in an apron. By Annie Jim.*

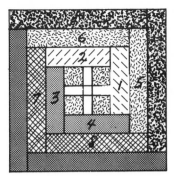

Fig. 89. Log cabin.

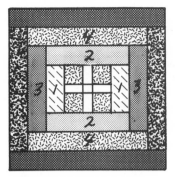

Fig. 90. Courthouse steps.

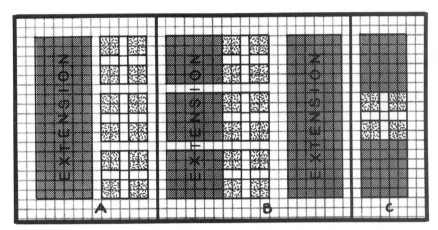

Fig. 91.

Fig. 92.

Fig. 93.

61

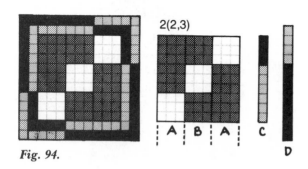

Fig. 94.

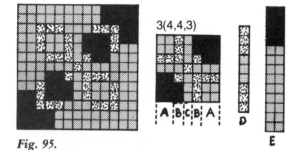

Fig. 95.

Figs. 94 and *95* both use the log-cabin method of surrounding a central unit, but segments C and D in *Fig. 94* and segment E in *Fig. 95* are placed in alternating positions to match colors at the corners.

Figs. 96–98 show a Greek cross. *Fig. 96* is a running repeat of adjoining segments; *Figs. 97* and *98* are crosses in different proportions with a central unit design surrounded by pieces joined in the log-cabin technique.

The patterns in *Figs. 99–101* are built on the same central unit as the Greek cross. The cross in *Fig. 99* has three surrounds of segments. The innermost segments can be cut from the same band as the outer segments, then trimmed. *Fig. 100* is a modern Indian turtle, with its central unit turned diagonally, trimmed at each corner, and two side strips added. To this, top and bottom, strips equal in width to the side strips are joined; then segments cut from two bands—one for the head, the other for the tail—complete the pattern. The central unit in *Fig. 101* is also turned diagonally and trimmed at each corner; three bands are made for the surrounding segments.

Analyzing these examples will help you create your own patterns.

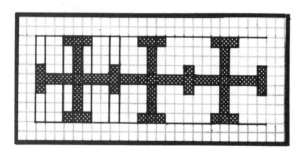

Fig. 96.

Fig. 97.

Fig. 98.

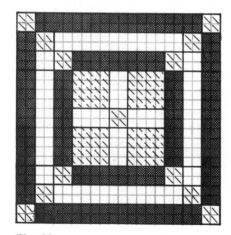

Fig. 99.

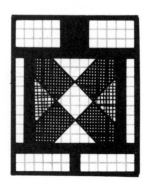

Fig. 100.

Fig. 101.

Figs. 102–113 illustrate Seminole-technique panels done as part of a project of the Unorganized Stitchers. Each panel was sewed by its designer, and each measures 2 by 4 feet (61 by 122 cm).

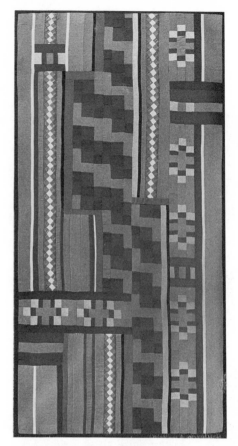

Fig. 103. *By Pat Albiston.*

Fig. 102. *By Jill Nordfors.*

Fig. 104. *By the author.*

Fig. 105. By Sue Roach.

Fig. 106. By Mary Ann Spawn.

Fig. 107. By Jo Reimer.

Fig. 108. By Lassie Wittman.

Fig. 110. By Edith Carlson.

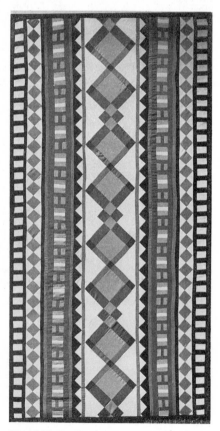

Fig. 109. By Barbara Meier.

Fig. 111. By Maggie Turner.

Fig. 112. By Eleanor Van de Water.

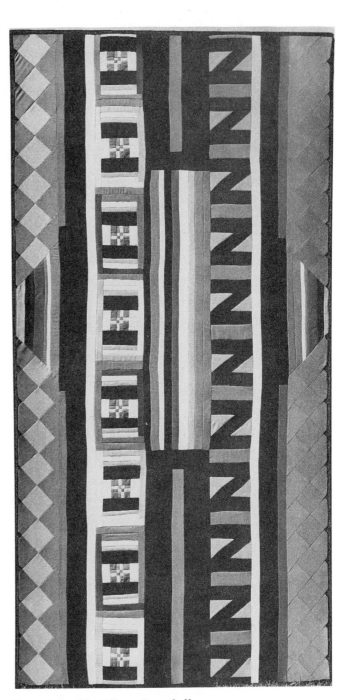

Fig. 113. By Flo Wilson Campbell.

Figs. 114–120 illustrate contemporary hangings by Carol Tate, combining Seminole and strip methods with hand-dyed linens, cottons, and silks. Machine-pieced and quilted.

Fig. 115.

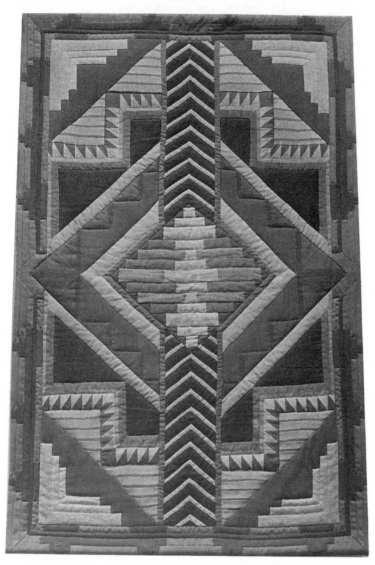

Fig. 114.

Fig. 116.

Fig. 117.

Fig. 118.

69

Fig. 119.

Fig. 120.

Contemporary Work

Over the years, you can see changes in style in the work of the Florida Indian women, just as there are changes in non-Indian styles. But the Indian variations stay within the traditional use of the patterns. Design sizes change, and the number of bands within a skirt or jacket will vary with the year, and color choices shift. Knowledgeable people can tell the approximate date of a photograph of Indians by the patterns and style of their garments. But the changes are slight, and an overall tradition is easily identifiable in the rows of horizontal bands.

It has been non-Indians who have adapted the patterns for quilts, banners, wall hangings, or trim on clothing fashionable to the non-Indian world. They use a variety of fabrics and colors and place their patterns in various ways. Their debt is apparent, but they have brought their own ideas and choices into play. This is as it should be. No true artist finds interest in merely copying another's work. The purpose of learning this technique is not to duplicate the Indian styles, but to use their method as a stepping stone to original designs. It is the ingenuity of the Indian technique that makes artistic exploration in this direction possible. And perhaps someday a young Indian girl will find inspiration from contemporary non-Indian artists to take this work still further, to areas yet unexplored, or will find new ways to adapt her traditional work to non-traditional ends, producing art that will reflect her heritage in a monumental way. The circle of influence is never-ending.

Whenever possible, the artists whose work is shown in this book have shared with us something of how they work. In their plans, these artists have constructed elements by using traditional techniques and then have arranged those elements into new combinations. The overlap of Seminole technique and manipulation of the strip method is very apparent and is hard to separate. Some artists have used the strip method with a degree of preplanning for geometric patterns that is more typical of the Seminole work. In some works, the design elements could have been taken directly from Seminole instructions, but a change of scale and fabric give them a new look.

Enjoy this work as you would a gallery showing, noting ideas and influences. Then after you, too, have developed some skill in basic technique, think in new directions.

Contemporary adaptation can be found in clothing, personal or home accessories, wall panels, quilts for

Fig. 121. Nomad Dress *with satin ribbons sewn to sheer voile and cut in Seminole fashion to make each panel; mauve to peach tones with burgundy trim. Ribbon streamers ⅛ inch wide hang from the waist over the skirt. By Joy Saville. Yvonne Porcella pattern.*

wall or bed—even in Pat Albiston's boot spats (*Fig. 146*). While the patterns themselves are made by the same method (whatever their final use), joining them involves particular approaches because of the size and shape desired in the finished product. A rectangular wall hanging must be kept at precise angles in joining so that it will be a rectangle when it is finished. But the straight angles of patterns will have to be modified to fit around a flared skirt. Whatever their use, all patterns must be cut and joined with absolute precision to fit smoothly to the perimeter of the final design.

To plan contemporary Seminole work you must know what you want to accomplish and how you plan to use the finished product. A variety of projects are

Fig. 122. A-line skirt with border panels of diagonal patchwork. Each panel unit is tapered toward the top to fit the curve of the skirt. By Flo Wilson Campbell.

Adapting

Turning corners with a pattern band, or otherwise adapting it to a specific area, needs planning ahead. Adjustments may be needed to make a straight pattern fit into a sloped or shaped area or to arrange units evenly throughout a given space. A pattern band as a border of an A-line skirt may look straight, but it is not; it has been adjusted to fit flat against the skirt edge. There is no single way to adapt all patterns to all situations, so I'll mention several, and you will discover others. Notice, too, the photographs throughout the book. Many adjustments are obvious; others I have pointed out in the captions.

You can plan adjustments to scale on paper or calculate them with measurements or make up a short sample band and physically manipulate it, noting where adjustments will be necessary. You need to know two things: the specific size of the area you wish to fill, and the size and shape (whether unit or repeat) of your pattern. Once these two factors are clearly in mind, you will probably have a pretty good idea of what can be done. There are two areas in which compensation can take place: within the pattern itself, and within the surrounding strips. Most unit designs will be adjusted within their own seaming, but there are no rules. Do what works best for you.

To compensate within a pattern, you can cut any single segment wider or narrower to work out a measurement that will fit evenly within a specific space. Curves or fan shapes can be produced by a slight slant in seaming. Slanting inward, bottom to top, by only ⅛ inch (or a convenient 5 mm*) on each seam will decrease the upper width by 1 inch (and about 2 cm*) every four seams. Either straight or diagonal seams can be fanned out in this way.

Extra strips can be added around or between patterns. Many designs already incorporate spaces that can be varied in size or shape. *Fig. 123* shows wedge-shaped strips added between the straight bands on the yoke and the straight pattern band of the sleeve. Wedge-shaped spacers can also be used to adapt square pattern shapes to a flared skirt. Remember that a diagonally cut pattern band is on the bias and will be more pliable than a straight-cut one; and each can be an advantage at times.

Think ahead to corners or angles to be turned. Most patterns set in at 45 degrees will readily move around a 90-degree corner. Other angles can be trickier. A small mirror held upright at the same angle as is to be turned will reflect how the pattern will look if you cut and join at that particular spot. Move the mirror along and you'll be surprised at the variety of shapes you can

shown; the ones most often seen are clothing, wall panels, and quilts. Consider the following about your project: the size it will be, the shape of your design area, where it will used, and how it will be seen. If only seen from a distance, your design size and scale will surely differ from that of something meant to be held in the hands and enjoyed. Sooner or later, everything needs cleaning. Plan for it—keep your fabrics compatible. If the piece is to be displayed, provide for putting it up, for dismantling it, and for putting it away. A piece hanging in a protected place where it cannot be handled will need less cleaning than a piece on a wall at the head of a stairwell where it can easily be brushed or touched by passersby. Washing demands are different for something worn by a child for play than for something worn by an adult for dressy occasions. And some of us will do more ironing than others. Planning will be important to your success.

Fig. 123. Wedge-shaped pieces add shaping between the straight pattern band at the shoulder and the straight strips of a yoke. The bias of the shoulder band helps give a smooth fit. By author.

have if you join at different spots. Plan for the corners to turn at the spot you choose.

Some patterns will join at an angle more effectively than others. If you don't like what is happening at a corner, try using a piece of contrasting fabric and let the bands join into it. The entire corner can be pieced with a square cut from a piece of plain fabric or with a square unit design that relates to the pattern bands. Or a strip of fabric can be joined in or appliquéd over as a diagonal bar at each corner or turn. Another angle might be just the spot to use a triangle left over from cutting angle segments. Each space can have a life of its own. Look for new ways to add an imaginative touch at the same time you're solving a problem.

Keep It Flat

I'll start with flat work and finish with clothing. It sounds obvious, but flat work *must* be flat, and ensuring flatness may take some doing in several areas

of your work. A major downfall is puckered seams. In *Open Chain* (October, 1980), Robbie Fanning said, ". . . one reason the Seminoles pieced well was their use of ol' sidewinders [sewing machines with hand cranks on the right side]. . . . The hole in the needle plate was small, so the fabric was not drawn down in the bobbin case, which can cause puckering and uneven seam lines. You can duplicate their efforts by using a fine needle and fine thread in piecing and either a straight-stitch needle plate or a left needle position and a zigzag plate." Spray-starching the strips and pressing to a crispness before joining (as mentioned before) also helps a great deal. So does holding the fabric both in front of and behind the pressure foot, keeping it somewhat taut as you allow it to move through.

Because contemporary work involves using various fabrics, you will need to adapt your sewing techniques to the particular fabrics you use. When working with wool or moderately heavy upholstery fabrics, you may find little problem with puckering, but the bulky seams probably will not lie flat unless you use a ½-inch

Fig. 124. With planning, corners can be effective.

Fig. 125. Bargello #2, *92 by 96 inches (234 by 244 cm). Proportions were planned according to the Fibonacci series. By Maggie Turner.*

(2-cm*) instead of a ¼-inch (1-cm*) seam allowance. The extra bulk at the back of such a piece may prevent a flat look, so the piece may need padding, or perhaps quilting, to sandwich it together. Try a good steam-pressing first; you may gain flatness with care. When two seams cross, it means four layers of thick fabric must go under your presser foot. You may want to test before going too far. Obviously, the fewer seams in a design using bulky fabric, the fewer problems to deal with, so the first step is in the planning. Plan to use patterns in large enough scale that seams are at least an inch (2.5 cm) apart. That is, the smallest unit of your pattern design will be one inch (2.5 cm), and everything else will be scaled out from that.

Puckering may occur when fabrics of different weights are joined. If joining a lightweight and a heavier fabric, do as much of your sewing as possible with the lighter piece on top, where you can hold it slightly taut as you guide it through the machine. It's best to try such combinations with scraps before you start on your actual piece. You may need to make some tension adjustments or to baste before sewing. Be aware that good texture contrasts can be planned without great differences of weight. Heavy linen combines smoothly with suede in Carol Tate's piece in *Fig. 131.*

Joining the Sections

Flat pieces are built section by section. Some artists only roughly preplan their work. They begin by sewing and cutting up a few pattern bands and laying them out in one arrangement after another until they like the direction. Then they make any other bands or units needed to complete the design. Other artists diagram their designs carefully and completely on graph paper. Maggie Turner's *Bargello # 2 (Fig. 125)* was diagramed first, worked in sections, and joined without ever laying the sections out together; she saw it as a total for the first time after it was finished.

Whether your work is carefully or casually pre-planned, there is always the process of joining one section to another after each is sewn. And this usually involves some kind of work space—the floor, a counter, the kitchen or dining-room table, a folding cardboard made for sewers to use across the bed. Fiber artists are used to finding their spaces. A favorite work area of mine is half of a folding two-section Ping-Pong table. Over its top I place a thick wool blanket (or several lighter ones) topped with a sheet that has blue and white quarter-inch stripes. The stripes are lined up exactly on the square, and the layers are stapled to the bracing board that runs under and around the edge with a staple gun. The padding allows me to pin into the surface and allows flat ironing on its large area without damage to the table. The stripes serve as guides when I'm aligning the sections. A family that looks forward to a fast game of Ping-Pong, whether at home or at Grandma's, may frown on the table being off-limits for a while; it takes too long to get everything straight and secured to set it up weekly. With care, however, the table is in fine shape when your piece is finished, and it can again be open for games.

Whatever it is, you will need some flat space if you are to work well. You will also need a good-sized right angle or T-square and a yardstick to line up your sections precisely. If your measurements aren't exact, your piece may look just a little slanty as you work but completely cockeyed when you see it hanging on the wall. If sections are to be joined on the machine, be sure they are securely pinned or basted—and checked for straightness—before they are moved to the machine. Press each seam immediately after sewing; then return the joined sections to your work space and check again for straightness and flatness before joining the next section. It's much easier to make corrections right away than later when other areas have been affected by a slanting seam.

Proportions

Seminole patchwork provides two shapes to work with: continuous running pattern bands and square blocks of single pattern units. The Seminoles traditionally join their single units into bands and work entirely with horizontal rows of these pattern-unit bands. It is essentially non-Indian technique to use pattern bands at various angles, blocks of single pattern units alone or in repeats other than horizontal, or areas of Seminole mixed together with areas of appliqué or strip patchwork.

In planning contemporary work, you must decide not only the size of the patterns to be used but also their size in proportion to the overall piece and their placement within its perimeter. Visual impact is determined by scale, and control of scale is one of the artist's most valuable tools. The amount of time and the amount of material needed to make any item is determined by both its overall size and the scale of the internal patterns. An intricate pattern of small segments can take more time to make and loses proportionally more material to seam allowances than a somewhat larger pattern.

How wide should each band be? How close together should the rows be? Lassie found that by applying to measurements the progression of numbers developed by thirteenth-century mathematician Leonardo Fibo-

nacci, even beginners to art can arrive at pleasing proportions in their work.

The Fibonacci series is a progression of numbers in which each number is the sum of the two numbers before it: 1, 1, 2, 3, 5, 8, 13, 21, 34, 55, 89, 144, and so on. Fibonacci arrived at the series because he wanted to know how many offspring would be produced in one year if, beginning with one pair of rabbits, every pair periodically reproduced another pair. The resulting series surprisingly turned out to be a key to a great number of progressions, ratios, or proportions found in nature. The spirals of seeds in the center of sunflowers and daisies follow these proportions, as do the sections of pine cones and pineapples. So does the ratio of your head to your body and the ratio of one joint to another in your fingers. This series was found also to relate mathematically to the Greek golden section, long a standard of good proportion within a rectangle.

But knowing that such a magical series exists does not provide an automatic answer to your placement questions; it needs adaptation—translation—to the language of torn strips and pattern bands to be immediately useful. To make this adaptation, Lassie's students first write down the Fibonacci series vertically. Alongside this list, they write a second series of numbers, in inches, starting with ⅛ inch, as shown in *Fig. 126.* Work can then be designed so that each *finished* measurement (that is, without seam allowance) is one of the measurements found in the series. Invariably, each student is comfortable with his or her resulting arrangement; it is pleasing and has a sense of balance. In the piece shown in *Fig. 128,* all measurements were chosen from a Fibonacci series starting with ⅛ inch.

Adapting the Fibonacci Series to Inches

Fibonacci Series	*Inches*
1 + 1 = 2	⅛ + ⅛ = ²⁄₈
1 + 2 = 3	⅛ + ²⁄₈ = ⅜
2 + 3 = 5	²⁄₈ + ⅜ = ⅝
3 + 5 = 8	⅜ + ⅝ = ⁸⁄₈ = 1
5 + 8 = 13	⅝ + ⁸⁄₈ = ¹³⁄₈ = 1⅝
8 + 13 = 21	⁸⁄₈ + ¹³⁄₈ = ²¹⁄₈ = 2⅝
13 + 21 = 34	¹³⁄₈ + ²¹⁄₈ = ³⁴⁄₈ = 4²⁄₈
21 + 34 = 55	²¹⁄₈ + ³⁴⁄₈ = ⁵⁵⁄₈ = 6⅞
34 + 55 = 89	³⁴⁄₈ + ⁵⁵⁄₈ = ⁸⁹⁄₈ = 11⅛
55 + 89 = 144	⁵⁵⁄₈ + ⁸⁹⁄₈ = ¹⁴⁴⁄₈ = 18

You can as easily assign metric measurements to the series; if one centimeter is taken as the smallest number, the Fibonacci series of numbers can be used as they are given.

Fig. 126.

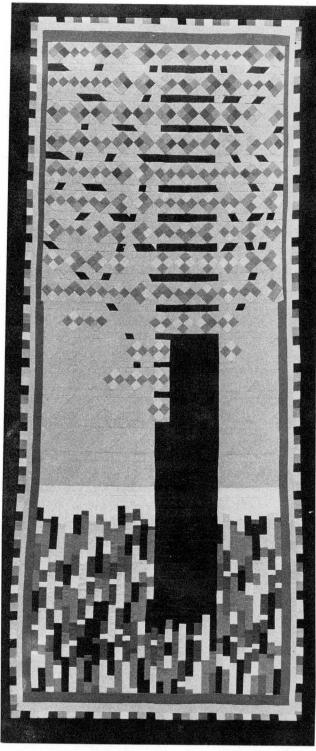

Fig. 127. Tree, *a wall panel 36 by 84 inches (91 by 213 cm), using Seminole patterns for leaves and irregular sections of strips for bark. By Flo Wilson Campbell.*

Scale can, of course, be altered by changing the assigned measurement; just use the same process. Start small enough to incorporate the smallest unit you will be working with. There is no upper limit to your series, and you can choose any numbers anywhere within it. It is important to remember that this series is a *guide* not a rule. It is intended to expand confidence and possibilities, not to limit them. Vary any space your eye motivates you to change. Your art is your personal sense of arrangement, your personal need to organize; it is successful if it pleases no one but you.

If you want to read more about classic geometric proportions in design, try Esther Warner Dendel's book *Designing from Nature* (Taplinger, 1978) for a brief but clear explanation.

Today's Artists

It's interesting to talk to highly innovative artists about their work. Their pieces usually transcend techniques used routinely, obvious colors, fabrics obtained from readily available sources, and other such "packaging" that would make them easy, or even possible, to duplicate. But the ideas of these people are a rich source of inspiration. I've shared what I can put onto paper—words and photographs—with you.

A number of Flo Wilson Campbell's innovations were inspired directly by our analysis of Seminole patterns. Like much other contemporary work, hers is a mixture of Seminole and strip patchwork. But the traditional influence was direct, and her excitement about what the Indians had accomplished was profound.

Rain Cloud (*Fig. 81*) has four areas of patchwork and several insertions of plain band, with a focal point of a growing rose of embroidery. The rose on this piece and the one on *Window Pane* (*color plate H*) were worked entirely with the Palestrina knot on a ground of double fabric. Two pieces of cloth were cut in the shape of the rose and sewn together, leaving an opening just big enough to turn the piece right side out. Edges were trimmed and clipped, the piece was turned and pressed, and the opening was blind-stitched closed. This doubled, finished shape was entirely covered with stitches, and the finished embroidery was blind-stitched in place on the pieced work.

Instructions for some of Flo's individual patterns are included with the diagrams. Techniques in her work that are of special interest are: her use of feathered edges created by tearing Kettle Cloth, the graduation of angles in *Receding Image* (*Fig. 78*), and the irregular mosaics of bark in *Tree* (*Fig. 127*) that set up texture and motion in a subtle way that seems random but is

Fig. 128. *Sampler of patterns proportioned according to the Fibonacci series, built on multiples of ⅛ inch. By Lassie Wittman.*

Fig. 129. *Wall quilt, 56 by 84 inches (142 by 213 cm), with Seminole patterns in large scale. Machine-pieced and quilted. By Marydel Leiter.*

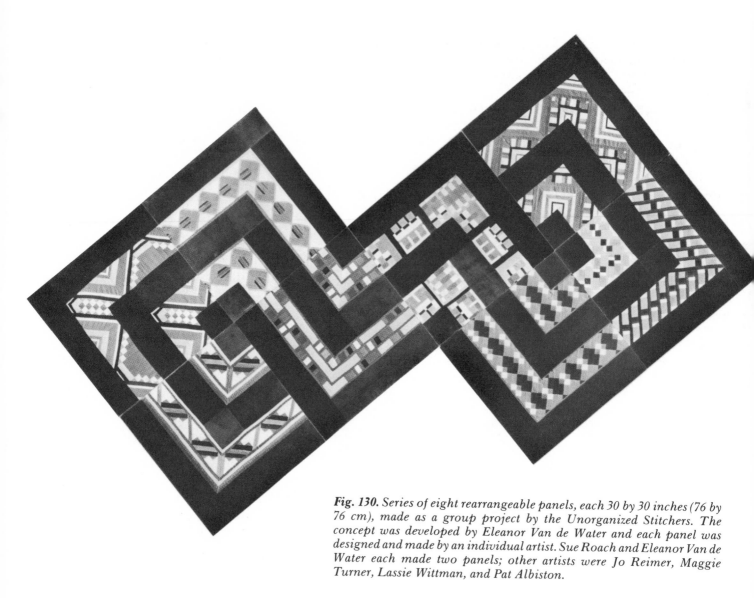

Fig. 130. Series of eight rearrangeable panels, each 30 by 30 inches (76 by 76 cm), made as a group project by the Unorganized Stitchers. The concept was developed by Eleanor Van de Water and each panel was designed and made by an individual artist. Sue Roach and Eleanor Van de Water each made two panels; other artists were Jo Reimer, Maggie Turner, Lassie Wittman, and Pat Albiston.

under complete control. Flo worked entirely in sport-weight cotton blends such as Kettle Cloth and Trigger.

The group of twelve wall panels shown in *Figs. 102–113* was the result of a rewarding experiment by a northwestern group, the Unorganized Stitchers (US). Wishing to use Seminole patchwork in a new way, they decided that stretched wall panels could create strong fabric graphics. Flo Wilson Campbell suggested and organized the project; twelve of the group chose to take part. Ground rules were agreed to and a committee of three selected and bought the fabrics. Each participant was given an identical packet of fabric pieces with which to design and make one 2-by-4-foot (61-by-122-cm) panel, unmounted. The individual artist could choose a small amount of a supplementary color but otherwise had to stick to and include at least some of each color provided. Design areas were to have no space wider than 3 inches (8 cm)

and none narrower than ⅝ inch (1.7 cm), and all were to have a vertical "feel."

Finishing was done as a group. Each individual brought her completed panel, and the finishing work was set up as an assembly-line process. The stretcher bars were prepared by stretching a piece of muslin taut over each frame and then stapling it there as a support for the panel. After pressing the panels carefully, one team measured, marked, and added strips of black Trigger cloth around all edges. The cloth was cut to extend one inch on the panel face and around to the back of the stretcher bars. Each panel was carefully positioned and stapled onto its own stretcher bars. Then another team blind-stitched a stretched backing of plain cloth to each panel and added a notched hanging bar to the top of each frame. The result was twelve individual works of art, totally unalike, yet complementing each other when together.

A design plan by Eleanor Van de Water was chosen by the US group for a second group project and can be seen in *Fig. 130*. This time there were eight participants to make the planned squares of black no-wale corduroy, each square 30-by-30 inches (76-by-76 cm) and slashed by two right-angle bands of patchwork in rust, blue, beige, and white fine-wale corduroy. Each pattern band had to be precise in width and placement to allow the squares to be hung together in a variety of arrangements. Ground rules similar to those of the other project were effected. Fabrics were bought and distributed as before. Each participant was to include some of each color provided. Strips were to be torn no wider than 2½ inches (6 cm) and no narrower than ¾ inch (2 cm). Corner seaming was to be consistent with instructions, and the measurement of the finished piece was to include enough fabric to stretch around the stretcher bars. The last sentence of the instructions read, "Accuracy is imperative." Eleanor did all of the mounting and finishing. Hanging brackets were mounted on all four sides of the frame, and Velcro squares were attached to outside corners of each square so pieces would stick snugly together in whatever arrangement was decided upon. This group piece was exhibited at a gallery in Seattle, in Needle Expressions '78, and was part of the travel show that followed.

Carol Tate (*Fig. 131* and *Figs. 114–120*) uses a number of fiber combinations in her work, often dying her fabrics to get the colors she wants. She especially likes to work in linen but also uses silk, cotton, rayon, and suede. The original inspiration for her pieced work came from a Seminole-made apron of her mother's. Fascinated by its pattern constructions, she explored similar techniques with fabric, but in her own way. She does not duplicate any Seminole patterns, but she uses their techniques to create new, strong designs for her own wall pieces, which are sought after by northwestern collectors. Carol is presently applying dyes and paint directly to cloth and cutting holes through the surface to the backing to gain dimension—work that is unrelated to her work shown here. As an artist, she frequently seeks new frontiers. Of the Seminole technique she says, "I still am fascinated by the almost endless possibilities it offers. It is a technical tool, basically . . . but has the potential of becoming much more with innovative use of color and the willingness to experiment."

Fig. 131. *Suede combined with hand-dyed linen, 26 by 26 inches (66 by 66 cm). By Carol Tate. From the collection of the author.*

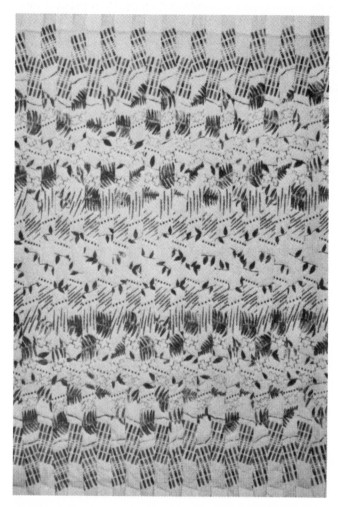

Fig. 132. Cimarron, *53 by 79 inches (135 by 201 cm), is cotton, printed by hand, cut and joined in Seminole fashion, and machine-quilted. By Margot Strand Jensen.*

Fig. 133. Seminole Cross, *50 by 64 inches (127 by 163 cm). By Joy Saville, who used cotton calico, machine-stitched and quilted, and Seminole methods in a contemporary manner. From the collection of Beth and Mark Berman.*

Cimarron (Fig. 132), by Margot Strand Jensen, is another piece in which the fabric is unique. Margot hand-printed ten yards of cotton with strips of leaves, ferns, crosses, and bars; then she cut the yardage into diagonal segments and joined them in the typical Seminole manner. Machine-quilted, it hung in Needle Expressions '80.

Joy Saville used cotton calicoes for her machine-stitched and quilted *Seminole Cross (Fig. 133)*. She joined her pieces in the usual way, but the scale, color, and placement make the work most unusual. Joy made the angles of her cross first, then filled in for color and balance. She writes, "I continue to be fascinated by the variety of design possibilities with Seminole patchwork . . . exploring the illusiveness of color, showing depth and movement. . . ."

Helen Bitar has long been known in the fiber field for her forceful use of bright, clear colors and her

interesting shapes (*Fig. 134*). And it is precisely these two characteristics that give so much power to her own approach to Seminole patchwork. The color that becomes art when Helen uses it is the castoff color of someone else. She gets her fabrics at the Goodwill. They are new, not used, fabrics—material that was once bought for sewing that never got done, and that was finally discarded. She looks for pure, bold color. The kind of fabric is secondary, and she uses cottons, synthetics, sometimes corduroy, or even a bit of satin. She works entirely by "feel," introducing certain color combinations into various patterns, trying different ones until she has a basketful of trial pattern-band pieces. Spreading her pieces out, she shifts them into various arrangements until a direction begins to grow. Starting at the center, she arranges outward, and the idea takes on a life of its own. Often more sewing, or even more shopping, will be necessary to carry out the

Fig. 135. Quilted Bargello #1, *34 by 27 inches (91 by 69 cm). The proportions of this work, which is machine-pieced and quilted, were determined by the Fibonacci series. By Maggie Turner.*

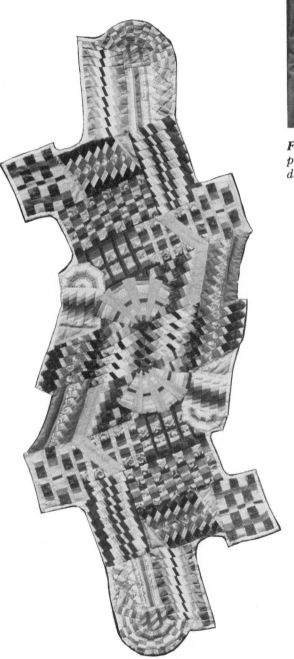

Fig. 134. *Contemporary wall piece, 42 by 83 inches (107 by 211 cm), combining sections of Seminole pattern bands. Backed and machine-quilted. By Helen Bitar.*

evolving piece. Areas are joined by machine, and once the entire shape has been joined, it is padded and quilted. Multiple loops are attached to the back of the piece to hold the projecting points. There's no hint of rejects in these powerful pieces.

Maggie Turner's interest in Seminole patchwork led her to a strip quilt, *Quilted Bargello #1 (Fig. 135).* Having seen bargello patterns based on quilt designs, she thought it was time to work the other way around. When making the ten-strip bands, she made half of them with extra width on the top strip and half with extra width on the bottom strip. This allowed her to shift the segments up or down for the pattern. The widths of the segments follow the Fibonacci series and are 1-, 2-, 3-, and 5-inch (2.5-, 5-, 7.5-, and 12.5-cm) widths. Maggie completely diagramed the piece first, figuring yardage and making all seams according to her diagram. The piece was worked in three sections to allow manipulation in the machine, and it was never laid out flat as it was joined and quilted. Padded, then quilted within the seams with the stich-in-the-ditch method, the quilt was shown in Needle Expressions '80.

Michael James is a nationally known quilter and author who has also found Seminole technique interesting. He has made several pieces incorporating the traditional patterns. The strip patchwork *Quintet*

Fig. 136. Quintet, *68 by 68 inches (173 by 173 cm), machine-pieced and hand quilted. By Michael James.* © *1980.*

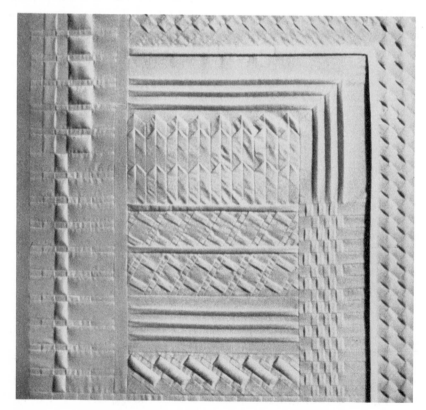

Fig. 137. *All white muslin, tucked, pieced, and stuffed to form three-dimensional white-on-white Seminole patterns. By Jill Nordfors.*

Fig. 138. *Two studies by Donna Prichard. Each uses two bands made from six strips, dark to light in value. (Top) Straight cuts of irregular width; (bottom) irregular angles. Edges are shown unfinished to indicate the amount of shift for placement.*

(*Fig. 136*) is machine-pieced, hand-quilted, and alive with motion because of the artist's sophisticated use of line and value. The dramatic sense of perspective and illusion that can be created with both the strip and Seminole methods is among the most exciting of their possibilities.

For the movement seen in *Broken Circle* (*color plate F*), Lassie cut segments of even width but spaced them apart at increasing angles. The tops of the segments touch, but each fans out so that they are 3 to 4 inches (8 to 10 cm) apart at the bottom, creating the semicircular effect. The alternating spacers' color values graduate from lighter to darker, as do those of the strips, achieving the effect of radiating light.

Another strip piece that conveys strength through the use of values is the wall quilt *Blue Stripes* (*Fig. 15*) by Donna Prichard. Squares were made from strips and sorted by color and value. When Donna tried to arrange them according to her sketched plan, "they seemed to resist." Laying them out on the floor she found a new arrangement, "as if the design were inherent in the numbers and values. . . ." The colors are mostly blues, with reds for accents, all in lights and darks of a wide assortment of fabrics.

Two of Donna's fabric studies are shown in *Fig. 138:* one with segments cut at irregular angles and adjusted to fit; the other with irregular widths arranged for interesting value placement. Each study uses two six-strip bands of light to dark values. The amount of offset can be seen by the edges left unfinished for the photograph.

Flo Wilson Campbell, the Unorganized Stitchers group, Carol Tate, Michael James, Joy Saville, Jane Lang Axtell, and Helen Bitar are among the artists whose Seminole work has been accepted and shown in national art exhibitions. Both Jane and Joy were invited to, and did, show their Seminole art in one-person exhibitions in April, 1981: Joy at the Works Gallery in Philadelphia, and Jane at the Textile Museum in Washington, D.C. None of this non-Indian work could be mistaken for the work of the Seminoles; it is Seminole technique gone free.

Seminole-made work is beginning to be recognized too. Several national magazines have had glossy spreads featuring Indian patchwork. But too often the patchwork is shown in colors chosen by the magazine's art director, which distorts the uniqueness of the Indian work.

A major acknowledgment of the value of Seminole work was the 1980 commissioning of a 5-by-10-foot (152-by-300-cm) sampler of traditional patterns made by Mrs. Howard Osceola (*color plate J*) that was hung in the Miami offices of the Federal Reserve Bank. The commission was instigated by Dorothy Downs's article on Seminole clothing in *American Indian Art Magazine* (Summer, 1979). It has led, in turn, to a commission by Westinghouse for four similar panels of the same size. Attention is growing.

At the same time, fewer of the young Seminole women show the interest to carry on their exciting artistic heritage. Only a few show the spark—may their number increase!

Fig. 139. Moonbeams, *65 by 46 inches (165 by 117 cm). By Joy Saville.* © *1980.*

Other Fabrics

"Unsuitable" fabrics are a good challenge. A thick or stiff material will need a design scaled large enough to keep the bulk of the seams to a minimum. Stiff fabrics that do not ravel can be joined with the cut edges butted together and held by top stitching. Metallics can be effective in the tiny mosaic squares in patterns, but plan to finger-press or use an iron with little or no heat. Sheers can have a stained-glass effect when put in front of light.

Geometrics have always been a popular design style, and Seminole patterns are beautiful as design alone. A painter, a metalworker, and a stained-glass artist can each find design ideas from the patterns. For us fiber folk the designs are a gold mine of possibilities. Any counted-thread work is a natural for the patterns because the squares of the canvas or cloth relate directly to the unit squares of the diagrams. The canvas work shown in *Figs. 142* and *143* is by Carol Frumhoff, who adapted ideas from photographs of the first panels made by the Unorganized Stitchers.

Fig. 140. Time Warp, *82 by 94 inches (208 by 239 cm), a "controlled explosion" of Seminole pattern bands. By Joy Saville.* © *1980.*

Fig. 141. *Detail of* Time Warp.

Fig. 142. Mounted box shape of Seminole patterns adapted to canvas work. By Carol Frumhoff.

Fig. 143. Exploration of Seminole patterns against backgrounds of stitches and pulled thread, on canvas. By Carol Frumhoff.

She uses the patterns against different backgrounds to set them off: stitched textures for some and pulled canvas for another.

Ultrasuede is shown worked in two ways. Edith Carlson has joined segments of the synthetic suede in the conventional manner, turning seams to the inside. She chose patterns that were not too small for its stiffness and combined the several colors of Ultrasuede with a compatible-weight black wool for the skirt shown in *color plate B*. Julie Goetsch did some experimenting and came up with an unusual method for her Seminole pattern in Ultrasuede (*Fig. 144*), a project that started with the purchase of canvas squares painted with charming Southwest Indian pottery designs that she wanted to incorporate in a skirt. For her patchwork border, she first cut with pinking shears five long strips from three colors of Ultrasuede and laid them out in parallel rows along a strip of poly-organdy wide enough for the five strips. She held them in place with Glue Stic and then permanently stitched them in place, using clear nylon thread along each edge. This produced a five-strip band, which was then cut into ¾-inch (2-cm) segments, cut with straight, not pinking, shears. The segments were lined up at angles along a strip of fusible interfacing and steam-pressed into place. The finished band was used full width between the needlepoint squares; it was cut lengthwise into two strips for the other edging on the skirt and vest.

Leather is heavier and harder to cut and manipulate than its synthetic cousins, but Pat Albiston adapted Seminole patterns to a leather vest and a pair of boot spats (*Figs. 145* and *146*). She wanted to lengthen the brown leather vest, so she inset a red leather pattern band with unit designs of brown leather and natural chamois. Each design piece was top-stitched in place; then the segment containing each pattern unit was conventionally seamed. Seams were pressed open, using heavy brown paper for a pressing cloth, then held back permanently with glue. In the challenge of the leatherwork, Pat forgot that when she was ready to return the lining to the now longer vest, the lining would need to be longer too. It was a problem she happily solved by adding an inside band of patchwork in compatible colors.

Pat cut her boot spats out of heavy, black canvas. Her next step was to cut paper patterns of the Seminole design she planned to use and to experiment with them. She settled on the use of one pattern cut in two sizes, the larger on top and a leather tassel extending from the smaller one at the bottom. Leather can be cut with scissors or an X-acto knife; Pat suggests the knife, especially for corners, to prevent stretching the leather. Dyed leather will show undyed edges when cut; these may be colored with a perma-

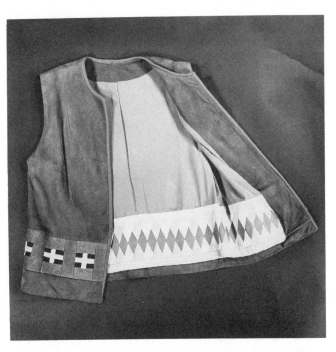

Fig. 145. *Leather vest with leather patchwork inset. Compatible pattern adds interest to the lining. By Pat Albiston.*

Fig. 144. *Seminole patchwork made by bonding Ultrasuede strips to fusible backing and cutting into segments. By Julie Goetsch.*

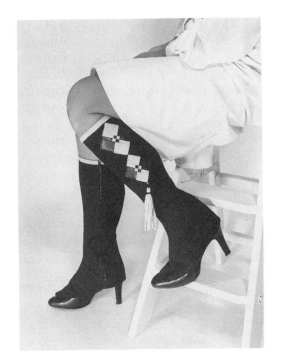

Fig. 147. *Traditional pattern, but an untraditional use of lace and ribbon in the original band. By Elizabeth A. Schimitschek.*

Fig. 146. *Canvas bootspats accented with Seminole unit design of leather and leather tassel. By Pat Albiston.*

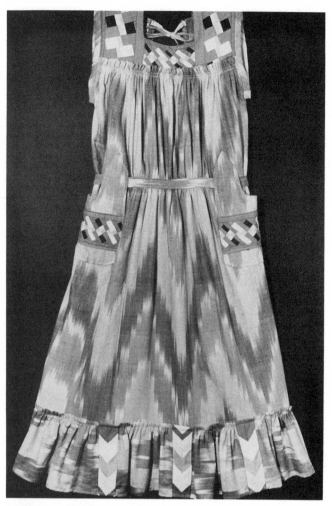

Fig. 148. The soft edges of purple and gold cotton in an ikat weave are picked up in the crisp edges of patchwork in the same colors. Note the chevrons added to the bottom flounce. By Jane Lang Axtell.

nent marker. Leather cannot be pinned (Ultrasuede can but may be difficult), so the pieces were held in place by double-sided tape. Each piece was top-stitched, using a roller foot and a beveled needle on the machine. After the designs were sewn in place, the rest of the spat was finished.

A change of materials may lead to a change in methods or scale. The designs are strong and can be used and combined in many new ways. Rather than wrestle with the difficulties of problem fabrics, you may want to work out your patchwork areas with familiar cottons or cotton blends and then insert or appliqué these areas to a garment or construction of a less workable fabric. Cottons or blends may also give you a better color selection than some other fibers, and their fine, firm weaves give you complete freedom to choose which patchwork pattern to do. Both velveteen and wool limit you to simpler or larger-scale patterns

because they are bulkier than cotton. However, a bright border of cotton patchwork, set off by a narrow band of colored fabric or ribbon, can be most effective against a plain wool or a velveteen base. Choose fabric combinations with an eye toward visual compatibility. The difference in fabric weights in the examples discussed causes no problem because a lighter, firmer fabric is being put on a heavier one.

Care of fibers used together should also be considered—their washability and their temperature requirements for pressing should be similar. A band that will need frequent pressing should not be used next to a metallic that will melt with minimum heat. As long as the entire piece can be handled and treated according to its most delicate fiber, all will be well.

Prints

Before they developed patchwork patterns, Seminole women used printed fabrics for clothing and added a narrow line of appliqué and a ruffle for embellishment. But Indian patchwork itself has always been done with plain fabrics. Having examined the wide variety of work being done by non-Indians who sometimes work in prints, Lassie and I feel that while Seminole patchwork can be worked, and often quite charmingly, in printed fabrics, these fabrics can create some problems. For one thing, many of the prints give a product a colonial look. For another, they do not produce the mosaic effect that is so much a part of the appeal of the traditional work. A print can overwhelm or defeat the intricacy of the pattern unit itself. Since the ingenuity of the construction is so fascinating, we hated to see it diminished. Naturally, some prints will be successful. But for this book, work that most clearly shows off the excitement of the technique is emphasized, and that work is most often done with plain fabrics.

In considering prints for patchwork, I believe most people think of the small, overall prints so often used for quilting. However, quite dramatic results can occur with the use of bold, modern prints; and stripes can be cut as though they were sewn bands, with interesting results. Jane Lang Axtell effectively used a print with an elephant motif (*Figs. 150, 189* and *color plate L*). She cut segment pieces from the print fabric in such a way that the elephants (and once in the same band, a palm tree for surprise) were incorporated into the pattern band at regular intervals. A border of hard-edged Seminole mosaic was set against the characteristically soft edges of an ikat weave. So, certainly, prints can be used with great success. But at the start, your strongest work is most likely to be done with plain fabrics.

Fig. 149. Prints used together in good contrast. By Caryl Rae Hancock.

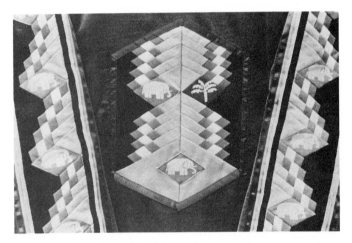

Fig. 150. Detail of print fabric incorporated in a dress as segments, adding interest in the repetition of pattern. By Jane Lang Axtell.

Fig. 151. Wall panel of Seminole patchwork using print fabric. Strong value contrast keeps patterns distinct. By Helen Russell.

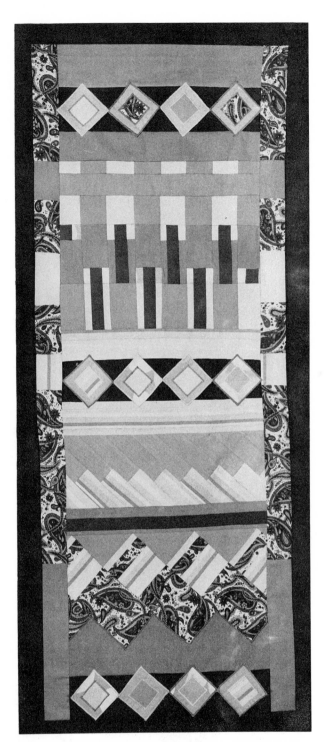

Fig. 152. First experiment with Seminole technique by Constance Howard. Print fabric, appliqué, and overcast cut edges add to its uniqueness. Diamond shapes are attached separately, with open space around them. From the collection of Jo Reimer.

Projects

The main purpose of this book is to be a guide to the patterns themselves. But I couldn't resist taking a peek at some of the ways you can use your patterns.

Commercial pattern books are not limited to clothing. Look in the back sections for patterns for all styles and sizes of hats, handbags, and belts for yourself, children, or babies. There are stuffed toys and stuffed furniture, bed and bath linens, holiday and house projects. Keep an eye open to projects that provide good areas for patchwork.

Of course, quilts are a natural way to use any patchwork, and there are numerous good books available on the subject. Look for one with instructions general and comprehensive enough to be useful with any pattern. I can recommend *The Complete Book of Machine Quilting* by Robbie and Tony Fanning (Chilton, 1980) or, for hand quilters, *The Quiltmaker's Handbook* by Michael James (Spectrum, 1978).

Pillows and Christmas ornaments are but two sizes of the same process, and both can provide a good way to try new patterns. Like the Seminole woman who sews up a patch of any new pattern she sees, you can sew up pattern samples and turn them into simple stuffed ornaments. Or fill them with hair or wool (to keep pinpoints sharp) and use them as pincushions. Neat rows of patterns that could have been a sampler

Fig. 153. (Top) Pillow with Seminole pattern bands. By Cheri Burt. (Bottom) Strip patchwork influenced by oriental tree-of-life designs. By Phyllis Bradfield.

Fig. 154. Pillows of Seminole and strip patchwork. By Jean Affleck.

Fig. 155. *Christmas tree made bright with Lassie's collection of Indian-made dolls and her own patchwork ornaments.*

Fig. 156. *Santa door decoration, 16 inches (41 cm). Designed by Natalie Szramek (Patch Press) and made by Pat Albiston, with added Seminole trim on hat. The tree ornaments highlighted with silver lamé are by Lassie Wittman.*

were made into a pillow by Cheri Burt (*Fig. 153*, top). Phyllis Bradfield (*Fig. 153*, bottom) ventured to a strip pattern with an oriental tree-of-life influence. The tiny, decorative braid trim is of small diamond shapes, similar to larger versions of Seminole.

Lassie's handbags (*Fig. 157*) feature detachable flaps, making it easy to change them to colors or patterns that best fit her day's outfit. You can make a similar handbag in any simple bag shape that is meant to have a flap. Commercial patterns are available, and it's not hard to devise your own paper patterns. Upholstery fabrics or Ultrasuede make durable bags. Cut and assemble your bag according to its pattern instructions, but do not secure the lining to the outer bag along the top of the back. Instead, machine-stitch the hook side of a strip of Velcro full length along the inside top of the outer fabric. Stitch its matching loop side along the inside top of the lining fabric.

Construct and line your flap (one side is patchwork, the other the bag fabric) to fit this opening exactly. A lightweight padding or stiffening can be added if needed. Finish the flap's joining edge by stitching along its full length two strips of Velcro, one front and one back, coordinating the hook and loop sides to the Velcro already on the bag. One strip can be sewn by machine, but the last will need to be stitched by hand. Hook the Velcro on the flap to the Velcro on the bag. Several flaps can be made for the same bag.

Fig. 157. *Shoulder bags with detachable flaps held with Velcro, allowing wearer to change flaps for other designs or colors. By Lassie Wittman.*

Fig. 158. *Critters made bright with strip and Seminole patchwork. The long lizard measures about 30 inches (76 cm). By Phyllis Bradfield.*

The stuffed animals (*Fig. 158*) are ones from a series done by Phyllis Bradfield, who designs and makes them, adding bright touches of Seminole and strip patchwork. You may decide to choose something like Phyllis's padded butterfly (*Fig. 159*) with wings of strips of color as a beginning project. Lassie's version (*Fig. 160*) emphasizes her Seminole work: the bright, double sets of wings showing Seminole angle segments, and the quilted circles adding dimension.

Boxes are a favorite project with many and can be made in numerous ways. Wooden boxes can be bought with recessed tops for which pieced and padded inserts can be made, and existing cardboard boxes can be covered with stretched patchwork. Complete boxes can be constructed to be soft or firm, depending on the inner materials. Maggie Turner demonstrates a simple approach to box construction (*Fig. 161*). She joins six squares of stiffened, double-sided strip patchwork; the edges are blind-stitched together by hand. Such a box

can be fat and puffy with stuffing. It can also be made of "pillowcase" coverings pulled tautly over cut squares of cardboard; the covering openings are blind-stitched closed and then the squares are joined. This simple box concept provides lots of room in which to use your own ideas.

This is but a brief look at a few projects. There is no limit to ideas. Think big and make Seminole banners two stories tall, using ripstop nylon. Some hot-air balloons use the zigzag pattern familiar in Seminole work, each section as big as a man. Think strong and make hammocks or upholstery from canvas or duck. Think elegant and make tiny patchwork jewels of bright silks and shiny metallics. Think natural and use hand-dyed, hand-woven fabrics in strong designs or undyed wools in handsome patterns. Remember a change of fabrics, color ranges, and scale can make just one pattern into a dozen personalities.

Fig. 159. *Butterfly with a wing span of about 15 inches (38 cm). Antennae are made of flexible wire wrapped with frayed cloth. By Phyllis Bradfield.*

Fig. 160. *Butterfly. By Lassie Wittman.*

Fig. 162. *Seminole patterns in organdy let the light shine through and produce a stained-glass effect. By Lassie Wittman.*

Fig. 161. *Box construction of strip patchwork over cardboard squares. By Maggie Turner.*

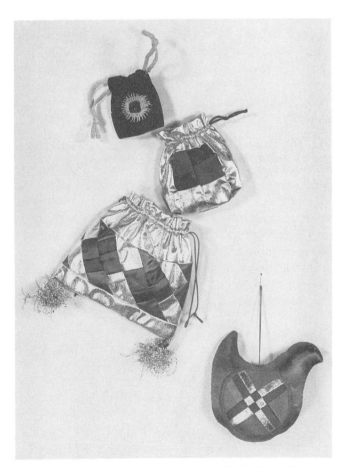

Fig. 163. *Bird ornament and three miniature bags that nest together use metallic cloth in Seminole patterns. By Pat Albiston.*

Fig. 164. *Sleeping-bag quilt by Anita Corum.*

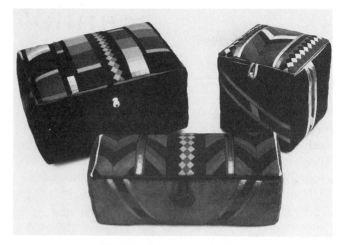

Fig. 167. *Boxes highlighted with Seminole trim. By Jane Lang Axtell.*

Fig. 165. *Patchwork made into glasses cases, small zipper purses, and a book cover. By Lassie Wittman.*

Fig. 168. *Placemat with Seminole trim. By Helen Russell.*

Fig. 166. *Baby bunting of quilted Kettle Cloth. The bottom pattern band goes entirely around the bunting, with two single motifs at the top front. By Nancy Wittman.*

Fig. 169. *Padded wall piece, 22 by 22 inches (56 by 56 cm). By Heather Price.*

Seminole Clothing

It's interesting to try to discover what outside influences contributed to the development of the unique clothing of the Seminoles. Dorothy Downs has been especially active in researching and writing about what influenced the garment styles. In her article "British Influences on Creek and Seminole Men's Clothing, 1733–1858" for the *Florida Anthropologist* (June, 1980), she goes into great detail about the Indians' first colonial contacts, starting with James Oglethorpe in Savannah in 1733 and his gifts of clothing and cloth to the important Indians of that area. In 1734, Oglethorpe took a group of eight Indians, including Tomochichi (a Creek Indian leader whom Oglethorpe had befriended) and his wife, Senauki, to England, where they met King George II and other important men. They saw sights they must never have dreamed of, ate new dishes, and were dressed in wondrous clothes. A painting of that meeting by Willem Verelst shows the Indian men in their finest furs and feathers, but Senauki wears a new dress. When they returned home, the tales of their adventures must have been hard for their people to believe, but they would have been impressive and so would the new, imported finery.

The next important contact came with the arrival, in 1736, of a group of Scottish Highlanders who settled near the Indians and got along with them extremely well. Dorothy Downs points out a number of affinities between the Highlanders and the Indians: both lived with an "elegant recklessness," were avid warriors, had a flair for drama in their speech and action, believed in a world of magic and supernatural spirits, had similar rituals, and had a clan family structure.

Of all the colonists, only the Highlanders wore skirtlike garments rather than trousers. By 1743, Indian men wore shirts acquired from the traders, but flaps "before and behind, to cover their privities." Shirts and cloth were on every trade list, but not trousers. It's not hard to see the similarity in dress of a Highlander—with his kilt, stockings and garters, coat and bonnet, belt and sporran, silver clan emblems, and tartan—and a Seminole. Painters of that era portrayed Seminole warriors in sashed dresses, turbans with ostrich feathers, broad, woven or beaded bands across their chests, and hanging tobacco pouches.

A lot of sewing must have been going on in the Indian villages, judging by the amount of cloth and the number of needles on the trade lists. The squares

Fig. 170. *Portrait painted in the 1830s of Tuko-See-Mathla, a Seminole leader. Clothing shows bands of pattern that was probably appliqué.*

and rectangles of bright colors that make up the tartans must have been to the Indians' liking. Through contact with the colonists of that time, the Indians would also have seen the patchwork and quilting the colonists were doing. One of the earliest patterns was the nine-patch, a pattern later used by the Seminoles. Runaway slaves who lived with the Seminoles must have brought ideas and pieced-work skills to their Indian friends.

Fig. 171. *Musa Isle tourist village photographed in 1923 by professional photographer Claude C. Matlack. Child above the dot is Mittie Jim, today a prominent patchwork artist.*

Seminole women make their own piece goods and fashion them into garments that are always made with rectangular cuts. Gathering previously made rolls of patchwork bands, a woman chooses how many and which bands she wants to combine and cuts from each band a length equal to what she wants the finished fabric to be. The bands are joined to make the fabric, and all garments are made from straight cuts from these joined rows of bands. The result is that, regardless of the garment—man's, woman's or child's—all patchwork runs in horizontal rows.

To make the Osceola garment shown in *Fig. 172* took ten feet (three meters) of piece goods, twenty-

eight inches (seventy-one cm) wide. Four pattern bands of ten feet (three meters) each were sewn together lengthwise, interspersed with plain bands of cloth of the same length, to make the twenty-eight-inch (seventy-one-cm) width. Rickrack and narrow strips of folded cloth were added for trim, and the piece was cut straight across into rectangles to make the sleeves, the bodice fronts, and the bodice back. As these pieced garment pieces are gathered and joined onto the yoke, their pattern bands continue in a straight line across the sleeves and bodice. This shirt, with its plain skirt, is called a transitional shirt.

Shapes of men's clothing changed more than

women's through the years. Paintings of Seminole men made in the 1830s depict them in knee-length, long-sleeved dresses of calico, kerchiefs around their necks, some with sashes around their waists and patterned bands or sashes held diagonally across their chests. Full-length portraits show leggings or gaiters worn on the legs, tied with patterned tie garters; feet are clad in soft leather moccasins. Scarves are shown wound around the heads, some turbanlike and trimmed with plumes, some with metal headbands.

British "plain shirts," straight and knee-length, were a popular trade item with the Seminoles in the mid-1800s and were copied in gingham and calicoes by the women, who added appliqué trim at the front neck openings. Over these shirts was worn a knee-length coat called a long shirt—reminiscent of the greatcoat worn over breeches by the Englishmen of the century. The Indian coat was of cotton, with a ruffle at the hem and a band of appliqué (later patchwork) just above the ruffle. In 1852, a daguerreotype was made of Billy Bowlegs, a Seminole prominent during the war years, wearing a calico long shirt with bands of appliquéd V's as a trim. Later this type of coat was known as the medicine-man's coat, a symbol of authority still used ceremonially today.

Sometime after 1910, patchwork began to appear. By 1923, an exhibition village, Musa Isle, was open to tourists. Here, Indians were fully dressed in the patchwork garments we have come to associate with them. Men wore the "big shirt," a one-piece, knee-length dress with full bodice, sleeves, and skirt, all showing rows of patchwork, gathered to join the rectangular yoke and waistband. Women wore their long skirts of patchwork gathered onto tie waistbands.

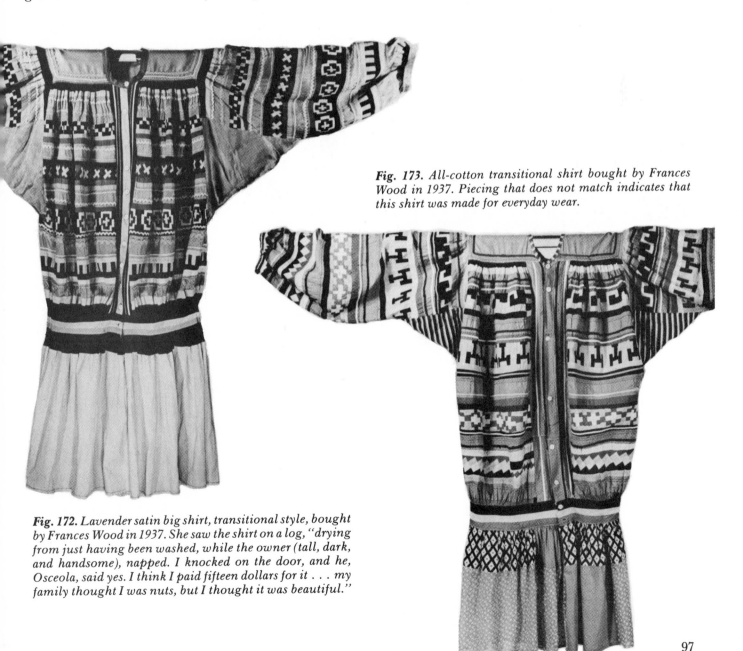

Fig. 173. *All-cotton transitional shirt bought by Frances Wood in 1937. Piecing that does not match indicates that this shirt was made for everyday wear.*

Fig. 172. *Lavender satin big shirt, transitional style, bought by Frances Wood in 1937. She saw the shirt on a log, "drying from just having been washed, while the owner (tall, dark, and handsome), napped. I knocked on the door, and he, Osceola, said yes. I think I paid fifteen dollars for it . . . my family thought I was nuts, but I thought it was beautiful."*

97

Their earlier midriff blouses with long sleeves and capelike collars had now evolved to capes gathered on yokes. They were long enough to cover the arms for protection against mosquitoes. A cape sometimes had a row of patchwork near the edge and was always worn over a blouse.

By the 1930s more bands of patchwork were being used on the skirts, but they were still rather wide. The traditional patterns of rain, fire, and lightning appeared often, but so did more and more new decorative designs. In 1928, the completed Tamiami Trail brought more whites into the area. Perhaps their example led most of the Indian men to begin wearing trousers. The skirt of the big shirt was often tucked into the trousers. This practice resulted in the development of the "transitional shirt," which had patchwork top and sleeves, but a skirt of plain fabric. It took less time to make and there was less bulk to tuck in, but it could still be worn without trousers. By the 1940s, the shirt had lost its skirt altogether and became the modern shirt, still with full blouse and sleeves, square

Fig. 174. Woman's cape of rayon gathered onto cotton yoke, worn over a skirt of the 1930s.

Fig. 175. Indian women in skirts showing the increasing complexity of contemporary Indian-made work.

Fig. 176. Skyjacket. *A child's jacket constructed from numerous extended bands, highlighted with a center pattern of grosgrain ribbon. By Poss Tarpley.*

yoke and added kerchiefs, but short and with a waistband, definitely meant to be worn with trousers.

For the Seminole women, 1935 to 1940 was the highest point of fashion: their hair was combed over elaborate frames, and they wore many strands of beads wound high and close around their necks. Synthetic fabrics had arrived, and rayon and nylon sheers were now used for their capes, which they wore over separate blouses. The bottoms of the capes were trimmed with lace and rickrack, but not patchwork. This period was also a high point in the invention of new patterns for patchwork, and skirts often had four or more bands. Patterns became smaller and more complex. One shirt of this period shows rows of intricate patchwork no wider than the regular-sized rickrack next to them. The work was being seen and appreciated, and the women responded with a flurry of activity.

But circumstances soon changed. With the boom of tourists in the 1940s, more and more women sewed for the tourist centers and to supply the roadside stands, so they had less time to sew for their families. Commercial goods were plentiful, and what little money they made from their sewing found many uses. Patterns became larger again. Everyday skirts got by with only one row of patchwork. More intricate sewing was done for festival clothes only. Other changes came along. In the early 1950s, collars were added to men's shirts, and the shirts themselves became less full and were worn more as jackets than as shirts. By the 1960s, many women were shortening their skirts to mid-calf length.

Recently there has been another flurry of new designs, especially among the Miccosukee women who have been developing intricate patterns with numerous extensions. They add rows and rows of narrow bands around a center pattern unit of traditional Seminole work. The additions are made with the log cabin or courthouse-steps methods used in quilting. Their rickrack sometimes follows the zigzag course of a diamond pattern; traditionally it was used only in straight rows. Color use is becoming more sophisticated—or perhaps they are now using color combinations more familiar to the rest of us!

Clothing Today

Seminole clothing is characterized by its rows and rows of horizontal bands of brightly colored patterns. Non-Indian use of the patterns in clothing ranges from inserting a single pattern unit as a decorative accent to constructing an entire garment of expanded pattern bands as Poss Tarpley did for *Skyjacket* (*Fig. 176*).

In this section, I will talk about ideas that may be helpful to you when you begin to incorporate aspects of Seminole design into the creation of your own garments. Most of the clothing illustrated in this book has been made or adapted from regular commercial patterns. But there are other good sources for garment shapes. Ethnic patterns by Folkwear offer a number of garments that can be easily embellished. They specialize in patterns of garments made before precisely sized paper patterns existed, when fabric was cut or torn into rectangular pieces and joined simply. Then, sizes were general—a child's garment was cut smaller than a man's, but it was big enough to accommodate growth. Clothes hung loose or were tied or sashed. Straight-cut garments have been universal throughout history and lend themselves to pieced areas, requiring little adjustments for curves. If this style appeals to you, you will want to see Yvonne Porcella's three books, especially the latest, *Pieced Clothing* (Porcella Studios, 1980). Her other books are *Five*

99

Fig. 177. *Man's square-dance vest, dramatic in black and white, with accents of bright red. It is unlined, except behind the patchwork area, for coolness. By Lassie Wittman.*

Fig. 178. *A 180-inch (457 cm) sampler is the flounce of this square-dance dress. By Lassie Wittman.*

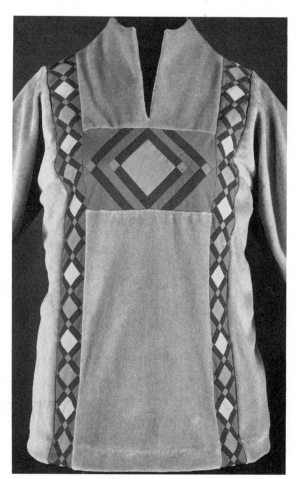

Fig. 180. *Corduroy jacket with Seminole patterns cut and joined so that contrasting grains of ribbing reflect different light patterns. By Lassie Wittman.*

Fig. 179. *Top of soft velour with pattern insets of cotton blend. By Lassie Wittman.*

Ethnic Patterns and *Plus Five,* also published by her own studio. The Max Tilke books *Costume Patterns and Designs* (Hastings House, 1974) and *A Pictorial History of Costume* (Hastings House, 1978) show a wealth of clothing shapes and ideas for incorporating pattern areas, but they give no measurements or explanations.

No one style of clothing is more right than another. Ethnic clothing does not fit in with everyone's life, but neither does designer fashion. Seminole patchwork can be a way to embellish, or it can be a decorative method of actually creating your own piece goods, out of which you can cut your garment. Decide what fabrics work well for you, what styles fit your life, how busy or decorative you like your clothing to be. Then plan your own one-of-a-kind fashion.

Lassie makes most of her Seminole clothing in cotton blends, and she *must* have one of the most outstanding square-dance wardrobes to be seen anywhere, with full, swirling skirts of Seminole patterns. One skirt (*Fig. 178* and *color plate P*) started as a sampler of patterns used by the Unorganized Stitchers for their first set of panels, and its 180 inches now twirl around her legs. Her husband has a vest to match each skirt. Lassie's soft velour top (*Fig. 179*) is highlighted by set-in slashes of coordinating cotton-blend pattern bands, a nice texture contrast with the pile surface. Her corduroy jacket (*Fig. 180*) is a masterpiece of light play; the pattern changes as she moves, light reflecting richly on each cut of the ribbed pile. Lassie works quickly. She "thinks" in fabric at her sewing machine as quickly as I do with pencil and sketch pad at my desk.

Two dresses of mine have been favorite experiments with fabrics. The gray dress (*Fig. 183*) is a fine wool worsted, inset with long bands of camel, black, and gray wool. Above the waist the strips have been joined on the diagonal leading into the diagonal pattern unit at the top. Space was left open for the belt to slide through, and the top are was lined and made into open pockets. It's a good example of single units made more important by the extension of plain bands through the entire garment. The other dress (*Fig. 184*) is 100 percent polyester with a silklike appearance. Both garments were designed to scale before committed to fabric. For the polyester, trial patterns were made to full size in cotton and fitted to the paper pattern. All adjustments were made on these trial patterns, and then the design was made in the final fabric. I designed both garments, Lassie made up the patchwork, and the garments were constructed by Josie Jewett while I was busy doing photographic work for the book.

To make *Skyjacket* (*Fig. 176*), Poss Tarpley constructed pieced work separately for each pattern piece. She first tore or cut a range of blue fabrics into strips 1

Fig. 181. *Square-dance dress. Notice that part of the square design disappears into the matching ground fabric, leaving the four-armed pattern "floating." By Lassie Wittman.*

Fig. 182. *Shirt to match dress in* Fig. 181. *By Lassie Wittman.*

Fig. 183. *Gray worsted wool dress with insets topped with Seminole-pattern pockets. Designed by author, made by Lassie Wittman and Josie Jewett.*

Fig. 184. *Silklike polyester dress with patchwork yoke and sleeve panel.*

inch (2.5 cm) wide and about 15 to 20 inches (38 to 51 cm) long. These strips were sewn into numerous bands. The order of their colors varied. Two-inch (5-cm) grosgrain ribbons that she had on hand were split in half lengthwise and sewn to make the rainbow band. These bands were then cut into long segments. Poss says that these segments could "be laid out and moved around . . . allowing for shading, variations in texture, and measuring." The design became firmly defined with the joining of the segments. Pattern pieces were laid on the pieced work with the overall garment design in mind, ". . . careful measuring was necessary to make sure the rainbow lined up." Original intentions to quilt the jacket were abandoned because the close seaming produced so much bulk. The jacket was simply lined with a cotton blend and snaps were covered to match the lining.

Experience teaches. Poss's notebook jottings from working on the jacket include these useful observations. For pieced work of this scale, strips longer than 15 to 20 inches (38 to 51 cm) caused problems by stretching and buckling, and even 15 inches (38 cm) was a problem on large garment pieces, such as the

Fig. 185. *The paper pattern shows sections of the cotton mock-up for the dress in Fig. 184 being arranged for placement, with a finished panel of polyester at the right. Designed by author, made by Lassie Wittman and Josie Jewett.*

Fig. 187. *Large-scale Seminole patchwork of brushed corduroy made into a vest. By Joy Saville.*

Fig. 186. *Full-length coat of pastel Kettle Cloth. By Taimi Dudley.*

back. Strips should be pressed before sewing, and each seam should be pressed immediately upon completion—pressed, not ironed. Seams do not have to be completely flattened. Repeated ironing of large pieces distorts them. The original fabric estimate was optimistic with this much close seaming. (She kept adding extra strips to the outside edges to make pieces large enough.) Trigger cloth and Clydella tore well; glosheen needed cutting. Grosgrain was very satisfactory to work with, of even width, and the ribs helped with crosswise alignment.

The full-length coat by Taimi Dudley (*Fig. 186*) and the vest by Joy Saville (*Fig. 187*) are two more examples of garments made entirely from patchwork. Taimi is the author of *Strip Patchwork* (Van Nostrand Reinhold, 1980), which includes some basic Seminole patterns. She fashioned the coat from large-scale rows of patterns made in soft colors of Kettle Cloth. Jane Lang Axtell is another who sometimes makes the entire body of a garment from patchwork.

Jane has developed a wholesale business in custom clothes that feature her unique use of Seminole patchwork, supplying craft galleries that include one-of-a-kind clothing in their shows. She employs a skilled seamstress, which leaves Jane free to design. She has printed sheets of outlines of her favorite pattern bands. These outlines can easily be filled with color, allowing her to explore a number of experimental combinations rather quickly. Of special interest is the juxtaposition in her work of large-scale patterns and tiny patterns in the same colors. The patchwork itself is usually executed in 100 percent cotton Rusticana, which she combines with handwoven cotton, wool, silk noil, cotton velvet, brushed denim, or soft blends of oriental ikat. Her work has appeared in noted galleries and museums, has been featured on TV talk shows, and was the subject of an article in *Fiberarts* (Volume 1, 1981). She is currently exploring ideas for combining patchwork with softer, more fluid shapes and fabrics as well as with specialized prints.

Jane's garments are sought by collectors and are timeless. As you develop your own techniques, keep in mind a beautiful "heritage" garment that you may contribute to posterity.

One-of-a-kind clothing made for exhibition and for sale. By Jane Lang Axtell.

Fig. 188. Black kimono inset with turquoise patterns of two different sizes.

Fig. 189. Dress with sleeve and side-panel patchwork, highlighted with oriental-style medallions in the center front. Detail of the print above can be seen in Fig. 150 *and color* Plate L.

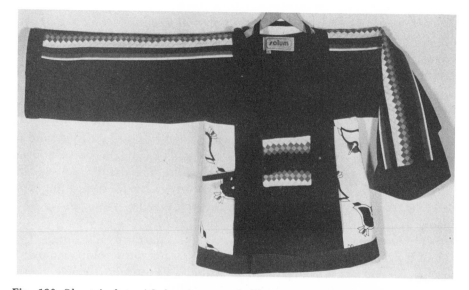

Fig. 190. Short jacket with hand-screened print as side panels. The sleeves and matching minibag are embellished with patchwork.

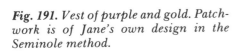

Fig. 191. *Vest of purple and gold. Patchwork is of Jane's own design in the Seminole method.*

Fig. 192. *Cape shows how variety within the same pattern can be achieved by combining segments from several bands.*

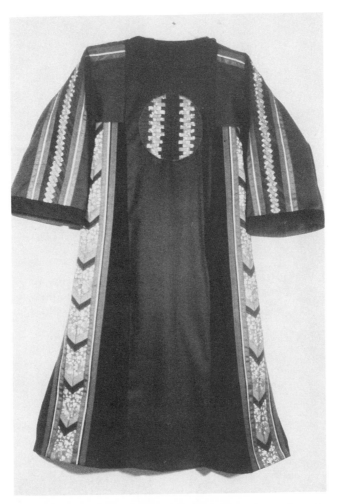

Fig. 193. *Dress with sleeve and side-panel patchwork, highlighted with oriental-style medallions in the center front.*

Fig. 196. One-piece square-dance dress with artist's own design on skirt. By Rosemary King.

Fig. 194. Dress highlighted with patchwork trim. By Lassie Wittman.

Fig. 197. Sampler of patchwork made into a jacket by Elisabeth A. Schimitschek. Both front and back panels are of bright pink, orange, and navy Kettle Cloth.

Fig. 195. Dress highlighted with patchwork trim. By Lassie Wittman.

Fig. 198. Patchwork yoke used to individualize a down vest made from a commercial kit. By Lois Nelson Valela.

Fig. 199. Cotton dress by Carolyn Caverly.

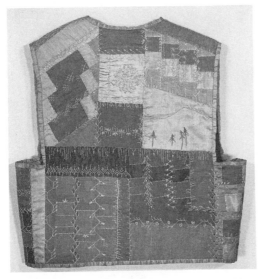

Fig. 200. Thai silk, pieced and embellished. By Jo Reimer.

Fig. 201. Jacket of Calcutta cloth with patchwork sleeve bands of cotton blend. The matching bag has a detachable flap. By Lassie Wittman.

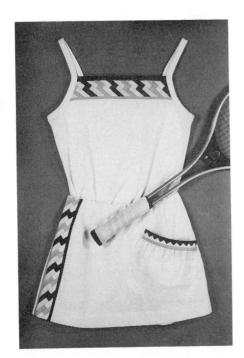

Fig. 202. Tennis skirt and top with bands of Seminole patchwork. Made by Rosemary King for Linda Peterson.

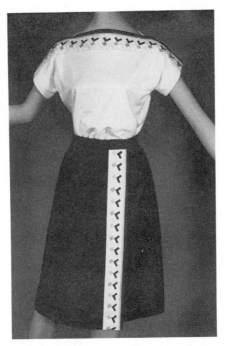

Fig. 203. Wrap skirt of woven sportweight cotton; T-top of cotton knit with matching bands of Seminole patchwork. By Rosemary King.

Fig. 204. Patchwork bib-yoke and bands set against a muted floral pattern, patchwork and print all in shades of blue. By Caryl Rae Hancock.

107

Seminole Women and History

Fig. 205. *Mary Motlow and daughter Bonnie in front of their modern home in Hollywood, Florida.*

History is told as the story of man and his wars. But what stories do the women tell? Who were the Seminoles, and what are the stories their women tell around the campfire? They are stories of settling new land; of bearing and raising children; of new things seen at the trading post; of men off again to battle, wounds and death; of packing, moving, and hiding; of making a new home without tools; of possessions lost in the haste of leaving; of relatives and friends leaving for the New Indian Territory—of their own men's refusal to go; of the husbands, brothers, sons wounded or killed, leaving their families and clans without leadership; of the final hiding, deep in the Everglades; of building a whole new life, a new culture, in these strange surroundings.

As settlers moved south along the eastern coast in the 1700s, the Indians pushed farther south ahead of them. Many members of various tribes in what is now Georgia and Alabama went south into the area that is now Florida. Although they shared the cultural manners, rituals, and ceremonies of the Creek nation, they consisted of two linguistic groups whose speech was related in structure, but mutually unintelligible. In the Spanish territory of Florida, individual groups tended to settle with or near others who spoke their own language; the Hitchiti-speaking people, called the Mikasuki, settled in the southern areas, and the larger group of Muskogee-speaking people, called the Cow-Creeks, settled north of Lake Okeechobee.

Regardless of their language groups, locations, or

Fig. 206. Grounds of Dania Indian Village, Hollywood, Florida.

original tribes, the white men called all of these Indians Seminole, a word of uncertain origin. In "Florida Place Names of Indian Derivation" (Florida Geological Survey, 1956), J. Clarence Simpson states that most authorities incline to the view that the name is a corruption of the Creek *ishti semoli,* meaning wild men. A popular but less probable explanation is that it comes from the Spanish word, *cimarrón,* which means runaway, or wild as a deer is wild.

Relationships with the European settlers were amicable at first, and the Seminoles lived a stable existence for several generations. A typical clan might live in a village with live-oaks, with crops and peach trees, and with horses and cattle pastured nearby. It might own two houses, one for sleeping and the other for a storehouse with an upstairs room used as a reception area or sleeping quarters for the men during warm months. Even then the women were good with the needle. Some of the villagers were black people, runaway slaves from plantations across the border. Some conflicts began because the Indians allowed these blacks to live with them in peace and would not return them to the whites.

As time went on, white settlers wanted more land for development, and in 1819 the United States bought Florida from Spain. Conflicts over land and slaves escalated, and in 1832 President Andrew Jackson ordered that all Indians be removed to the Indian Territory that is now Oklahoma. The Indians resisted

and a series of wars followed, but by 1860 most of the Indians were out of Florida.

Only a handful stayed, perhaps three hundred out of the once strong nation of five thousand. The resisters moved into the Everglades and the white men gave up their chase in order to fight another war. The Indians lived in the Everglades, isolated from outside contact, for about fifty years. Then once again white men came seeking more land, draining swamps, building roads, and changing the environment that supported the Indians.

Most Indians who sought refuge deep in the Everglades were from the Hitchiti-speaking groups. Although originally there were more Cow-Creeks than Mikasuki in Florida, they provided fewer leaders during the wars, and fewer stayed behind. The Cow-Creek Indians who left formed a strong Seminole nation in Oklahoma, and the Muskogee dialect continued to be their language. They had little contact with Florida, and they built a new life suitable to their new land, which is another interesting story.

But this story is about the Florida Indians and the patchwork that evolved during the years of isolation.

Only remnants of families straggled into the Everglades. So many men had been killed that much of the building of a new life fell to the women.

They had little but the clothing on their backs. Everything had to be built from scratch with materials that came from the land. Everything had to be easy to carry, for they were fugitives. They had to contend with the sub-tropical conditions of heat and water.

Under the circumstances, Seminole culture may have been better suited for survival than many others would have been. Even today, the Seminoles are a matriarchal society, with inheritance and descent coming through the mother's side of the family. Although she has little to say in tribal affairs, it is the woman, not the man, who heads the family. She owns the property, hut, utensils, and cattle. The clan camp is likely to be headed by a grandmother, her daughters, and their families. When a woman marries, her husband joins her clan and they live in her camp until, and if, they build their own camp nearby. Unmarried men are expected to look after their sisters and mothers until the men leave to marry. (Although no longer practiced, polygamy was a practical state among the Seminoles when the surviving men were greatly outnumbered by the women.) A young child is educated by the mother and brothers of its mother.

Instead of living in town with their log houses built around a square, as they had before, in the Everglades the Indians lived in family or clan camps. They built shelters called chickees, much like the shelters Florida's aboriginal Indians had built. Each chickee had a platform floor two feet above the ground, a roof

Fig. 207. Early canoe, hewn from a cypress log.

Fig. 208. Cooking chickee in a Miccosukee village along the Tamiami Trail. Cooking chickees do not usually have the platform floors found in other chickees.

Fig. 209. Annie Jim rocking her granddaughter to sleep in a swinging hammock in a chickee. She pulls on a scarf tied to the supporting ropes.

Fig. 210. *Its age is showing, but an early machine is still kept on a storage shelf in a village chickee.*

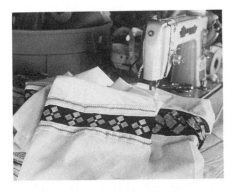

Fig. 211. *Today's Indian women use electric machines with commercial holders for large cones of thread, and they buy their cloth by the bolt.*

Fig. 212. *Annie Jimmie demonstrating patchwork construction at Dania Indian Village.*

Fig. 213. *Annie Jimmie's husband, Frank, now deceased, carving wood.*

Fig. 214. *Annie Jim with the same granddaughter.*

Fig. 215. *Dolls and woodcarvings made by the Florida Indians for sale to tourists.*

of thatched palmetto fronds, and open sides. Several chickees were clustered together, with one chickee set aside for cooking. Once an agricultural people, they now had dry space enough for only small garden plots and no livestock. For food they depended on what could be had by hunting deer and other small animals, fishing in teeming rivers, and gathering berries, wild oranges, guavas, and bananas. They hollowed out the ends of cypress stumps to form bowl shapes, where they ground their staple of corn gruel. Instead of paths for walking or horseback riding, they now had streams and swamps. To get around in the shallow waters, the Indians hewed long canoes, each cut from a single cypress log. Out of these years, the Seminoles developed a new culture and the new form of dress so uniquely their own.

There were always itinerant traders, and Indians would often travel great distances to barter. Before isolation, trade had introduced items from England, Spain, France, and America, and Indian women prized pottery, china, glass bottles, and mirrors. Some traders married daughters or nieces of chiefs and became clan members. English traders furnished guns to the Indians during the war years.

As the Seminole Indians were fighting their wars, the rest of the South was in increasing conflict over slavery. Just after the Indians went into hiding, the Civil War began. Before the war, the South had become the greatest cotton-growing region in the

world, spurred on by the invention of the cotton gin. Calico was one of the cheapest cotton materials made and would have been a staple to the traders. But at the height of the war, cotton cloth became extremely scarce. Cloth that had been easily available to the Indian women would now have been unobtainable. Like the white women they had so little in common with, the Indian women, too, would have had to learn to make do with whatever they could get. It would be natural for them, instead of making a complete garment of one piece of cloth, to mix any available pieces or join strips of leftovers. After the war, cloth production soon rose to, then surpassed, prewar levels, and the traders would again have brought bolts of material to the Seminoles.

For the years of the Indians' isolation, we have no record of what changes took place, but it is logical to assume that the scarcity of cloth led to some thoughts of piecing, though it was not until some forty years later that patchwork was actually seen. How soon after the Indian patchwork was first being made did anyone outside know about it? No one knows.

In 1871, on the south bank of the Miami River near the mouth, William B. Brickell built the area's first trading post. The Indians piled up their canoes with alligator skins and brought home powder, cloth, and needles. In 1896, the first railroad into Miami was built, bringing with it many changes. Suddenly more whites—tourists, settlers, and developers—poured into the area, building hotels and looking for land to develop. But the railroad brought something else. By 1900, hand-cranked sewing machines were available to the Indian women.

In 1898, John Marion Burdine built Miami's first store, and his father, William M. Burdine, pitched in to help him run it. William Burdine was an old Indian trader and knew the Indians' tastes. One of the first items of merchandise that he stocked was bolts of bright cloth.

Seminole women had long been making clothing of colorful cotton cloth, some print, some plain. They had also done geometric appliqué and simple piecing by hand. With sewing machines and an ample supply of fabric, the women sewed rapidly, and they began to experiment with new ways of making patterns. Their clothing had been made of rectangular pieces of cloth sewn together, the rectangles torn to size from the bolt of cloth. Now the tear sizes became smaller and were sewn together in long strips of two colors. These strips were cut and joined to form new patterns that were much more intricate than the earlier hand appliqué. The first patterns were bigger and simpler than later ones, and as the patterns became more intricate, the colors became brighter. When the Indians appeared in town in their new and colorful clothing, they found tourists eager to purchase it. The whites who had entered Indian territory on the new roads bought Indian crafts and brought them new income.

In 1928, the Tamiami Trail, a road across the Everglades from Miami to Naples and up the coast to Tampa, was officially opened. It ran directly through the lands occupied by the Indians. This road opened the interior of the peninsula to hunters, settlers, and cattlemen and greatly curtailed the free use of the area by the Indians. Their fishing and hunting, their lands and waterways were disturbed as the tourists ventured into what had previously been out of sight. But it also made possible the selling of souvenirs—the colorful patchwork, dolls, baskets, and carvings—at roadside stands. The women began to spend more and then most of their time making items to sell, rather than

sewing for their families. The isolation and seclusion of the Seminoles was now over. Yet, even today, they still highly prize and guard their privacy, and they still take great pleasure in doing their best work for the clothing the family will wear for the festivals.

Each year the Florida Indian clans still gather for four or five days of festival and the ceremonies of the Green Corn Dance. While the men and older boys prepare for their rituals and feasts and attend their ceremonies, the women tend the camp, prepare food as they chat and gossip, and oversee the girls caring for the younger children. Young children gather in the afternoon to learn dances, and at sunset children and young adults, both boys and girls, play ball. Whole families go to the early evening dances, the women dancing to the right of the men, away from the fire, the

Fig. 216. Drawstring bags of patchwork held on bases of sweetgrass baskets, typical of many available in Indian shops.

Fig. 217. Recently made man's jacket, unusual in its repeats of one pattern (lightning) and the use of only shades of brown with white. Made by Annie Jim.

113

Fig. 218. *Indian-made blouses for tourists.*

Indians on the Brighton, Big Cypress, and Hollywood reservations and surrounding areas. The Bureau of Indian Affairs office is at Hollywood (formerly Dania).

Two-thirds of Florida's Indians speak Mikasuki, the phonetic spelling of which became the name of the self-determined Miccosukee Tribe. In 1962, the Miccosukees petitioned the U.S. government for separate tribal status, which was granted. The tribe was incorporated and now has its own offices and an office of the Bureau of Indian Affairs at Homestead, twenty miles south of the Tamiami Trail. Until these recent incorporations, no true Seminole tribe or nation existed, although the U.S. government made treaties and agreements as if it were dealing with legal bodies.

Both tribes have built tourist centers, restaurants, and gas stations to accommodate tourists and bring in needed money. Tribal stores, as well as family camps along the Tamiami Trail, sell patchwork and other crafts. Tribal leaders have learned the white man's laws and deal with him on his own terms, and they win important concessions.

Like other tribes in this country, the Seminoles consider their reservation their own sovereign nation, exempt from certain state and local laws, and they sell untaxed cigarettes and run a highly successful and luxurious bingo hall that is open oftener, and gives bigger jackpots, than the state laws allow.

Although often related in blood, the Seminole and Miccosukee tribes are otherwise quite separate political entities. Any Florida Indian can enroll in either tribe; those who do not formally enroll are considered members of the Seminole Tribe. About one-half of the Seminoles chose to enroll with the Miccosukees, who are considered more traditional and conservative. In 1976, the U.S. Indian Claims Commission awarded the Seminoles $16 million in compensation for lands

children—some as young as four or five—bringing up the rear. Court is held at every festival to decide on solutions to problems that have arisen during the year. After the fasts, the ritual baths, and the ceremonies, the men and boys can eat from the new crop of corn, and another new year begins.

Recently, as during the wars, great decisions have been made. The once self-sufficient Indians who lived off the isolated land could no longer do so and were forced to deal more with the decisions, bureaus, and cultures of the white men. The Seminoles became an incorporated tribe in 1956, consisting mainly of

Fig. 219. *Paper patchwork patterns adorn walls of school on Big Cypress Reservation. In this classroom a miniature chickee stands in a corner as a playhouse, complete with patchwork dress-up clothing. The school is bilingual: English and Hitchiti.*

taken from them, a settlement of $.50 an acre. The Miccosukees have rejected the award outright, claiming they still own their land. The Seminole Tribe is fighting the settlement because it gives part of the money to the larger group of Oklahoma Seminoles who have received continuing government help since relocation. The money is being held in trust until an agreement can be reached.

The Miccosukees are the smallest recognized tribe in the United States. In rejecting their claims to any Seminole monies, they are holding out for deeds to the lands they have occupied—76,000 acres of the Miccosukee Reservation—and in 1975, they sued the United States for one-fifth of the state of Florida. With favorable decisions, Alfred G. Haut, credit and finance officer for the tribe, believes the Miccosukees have the potential for becoming the most affluent tribe in the country. Already, according to Haut, the tribe's chairman has obtained grants—not loans—for the tribe, and it is the only tribe in the United States to successfully manage its own grants without supervision.

The future of the tribes is in the hands of the children. Families are close, yet children are given a great deal of say-so in their own affairs, even about schooling. School is not compulsory. The school on the Miccosukee Reservation is bilingual (English and Hitchiti). The teachers are non-Indian with Indian aides. The Hitchiti language is now being written down for the first time, and tribal stories and games are part of the children's day. The school I visited on Big Cypress Reservation had cut-paper patchwork patterns adorning the walls, a child-sized chickee built like a playhouse in the corner, and baskets of bright Seminole clothing for dress-up play.

After sixth grade, students must take a bus to nearby towns where they attend regular schools with non-Indians. Most do not continue. The ways are not easy today, and there are problems with the Indian young, as with too many of today's young everywhere, as they try to sort out their own values in the midst of social confusion. Perhaps today's problems pose a greater threat to the Florida Indian's culture than the years of wars and hardships did.

Yet a Florida policeman notes the remarkable honesty of these young people and believes that the clan system makes everyone brothers and sisters. He has confidence that, in the long run, the Indian values of these unique people will bring them through their difficulties once again.

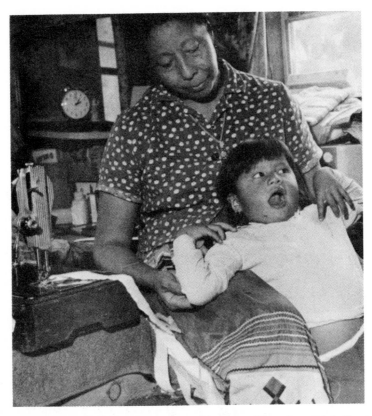

Fig. 220. *Mary Frances Cypress and her granddaughter Michelle at home on Big Cypress Reservation, where she showed us her sampler of 121 patterns.*

115

Where to Buy and See Seminole Patchwork

You can buy Seminole-made patchwork in various museums and ethnic gift shops around the country.

If you have time to explore the surrounding area of Miami, you can find patchwork and also see something of Indian life. Drive a few miles north of Miami on U.S. 441 to Hollywood, and you will see the Seminole Indian Village and the Seminole Arts and Crafts Center, both well worth a visit.

Heading west out of Miami on U.S. 41, you are on the Tamiami Trail and will see numerous Indian villages along the road. On this route we recommend these shops:

Everglades-Shark Valley Craft Center (26 miles west of Miami), P.O. Box 557205, Miami, Florida 33155

Miccosukee Indian Village and Culture Center (37 miles west of Miami), P.O. Box 440021, Tamiami Station, Miami, Florida 33144

Northwest of Miami, near Fort Myers, you will find the Immokalee Seminole Indian Reservation.

Other sources include:

Anhinga Indian Museum and Gift Gallery, 5791 S. State Road 7, Ft. Lauderdale, Florida 33314

Seminole Cultural Center, 5221 North Orient Road, Tampa, Florida 33610

The following museums have collections of Seminole patchwork, though these collections are not necessarily on display at all times. Other museums sometimes have a piece or two, which can be seen by request. Ask ahead about displays or for permission to study pieces privately. Membership in a needlework or quilting organization is often accepted by a museum as proof of serious interest, qualifying you for study permission.

Denver Art Museum, 100 West Fourteenth Avenue Parkway, Denver, Colorado 80204

Florida State Museum, Museum Road, University of Florida, Gainesville, Florida 32611

Heard Museum, 22 East Monte Vista Road, Phoenix, Arizona 85004

Historical Museum of Southern Florida, 101 West Flagler Street, Miami, Florida 33130

Museum of New Mexico: Museum of International Folk Art, 706 Camino Lejo, Santa Fe, New Mexico 87503

National Museum of the American Indian, 3753 Broadway, New York, New York 10032

Smithsonian Museum of Natural History, Constitution Avenue, Washington, D.C. 20560

Artists Whose Patchwork Appears In This Book

References are to figure number.

Bibliography

Your new patchwork skills may lead to more reading—for ideas on incorporating patchwork into clothing or accessories, for ideas on quilting by hand or machine, or for more information about the Florida Indians. Of the many good articles and books available, the following have been of special interest to Lassie and me.

ARTICLES

Buscho, Ann. "A Method to Her Madness." *Fiberarts*, November 1, 1981, pp. 31–33.

Capron, Louis. "Florida's Emerging Seminoles." *National Geographic Magazine*, November 1969, pp. 716–34.

_____ . "Florida's 'Wild' Indians, the Seminole." *National Geographic Magazine*, December 1956, pp. 819–40.

Davis, Hilda J. "The History of Seminole Clothing and its Multicolored Designs." *American Anthropologist*, October 1955, pp. 974–80.

Downs, Dorothy. "The Art of the Florida Indians." Exhibition Catalog from the Lowe Art Museum, 1976.

_____ . "British Influences on Creek and Seminole Men's Clothing." *Florida Anthropologist Society* (1980): pp. 46–64.

_____ . "Patchwork Clothing of the Florida Indians." *American Indian Art Magazine*, Summer 1979, pp. 32–41.

Evanoff, Betty. "Seminole Indian Patchwork." *Antiques Journal*, October 1975, pp. 50, 51, 56.

"In the Dark of the Swamp—Seminole Patchwork." *Fiberarts*, November 3, 1977, pp. 38–40.

McCane-O'Connor, Mallory. "Janice Billie: Seminole Patchwork Artist." *Flying Needle*, August 1980, pp. 18–19.

"Seminole Patchwork." *American Indian Hobbyist*, September/October 1959, entire issue. Out of print.

Tulloch, Valerie. "Patchwork from Strips." *Embroidery*, Spring 1978, pp. 24–25.

U.S. Department of the Interior and Indian Arts and Crafts Board. "Seminole and Miccosukee Crafts." *Smoke Signals*, Winter/Spring 1966, pp. 3–13; 21–23.

Wittman, Lassie. "Seminole Patchwork." *Flying Needle*, May 1978, p. 11.

BOOKS

Quilting and Patchwork

Bradkin, Cheryl Greider. *Seminole Patchwork Book*. Atlanta, Yours Truly, 1980.

Dudley, Taimi. *Strip Patchwork*. New York: Van Nostrand Reinhold, 1980.

Fanning, Robbie and Tony. *The Complete Book of Machine Quilting*. Radnor, Pa.: Chilton Book Co., 1980.

Gutcheon, Beth. *The Perfect Patchwork Primer*. New York: Penguin Books, 1973.

James, Michael. *The Quiltmaker's Handbook*. Englewood Cliffs, N.J.: Prentice Hall, 1978.

_____ . *The Second Quiltmaker's Handbook*. Englewood Cliffs, N.J.: Prentice Hall, 1981.

Johannah, Barbara. *The Quick Quiltmaking Handbook*. Menlo Park, Ca.: Pride of the Forest, 1979.

Laury, Jean Ray. *Quilts and Coverlets*. New York: Van Nostrand Reinhold, 1970.

Leman, Bonnie. *Quick and Easy Quilting*. Great Neck, N.Y.: Hearthside Press, 1972.

Puckett, Marjorie. *String Quilts 'n' Things*. Orange, Ca.: Orange Patchwork Publishers, 1979.

Wittman, Lassie. *Seminole Patchwork Patterns*. Rochester, Wa.: self-published, 1979.

Clothing and Accessories

Holderness, Esther R. *Peasant Chic*. New York: Hawthorne Books (American Elsevier Publishers), 1977.

Ladies' Home Journal, ed. *Creative Sewing*, New York: Van Nostrand Reinhold, 1977.

Porcella, Yvonne. *Pieced Clothing*. Modesto, Ca.: Porcella Studios, 1980.

_____ . *Five Ethnic Patterns*. Modesto, Ca.: Porcella Studios, 1977.

_____ . *Plus Five*. Modesto, Ca.: Porcella Studios, 1978.

Tilke, Max. *Costume Patterns and Designs*. New York: Hastings House, 1974.

_____ . *A Pictorial History of Costume*. New York: Hastings House, 1978.

Seminole History

Neill, Wilfred. *Florida's Seminole Indians*. Saint Petersburg: Great Outdoors Publishing Co., 1956.

Peithmann, Irvin M. *The Unconquered Seminole Indians*. Saint Petersburg: Great Outdoors Publishing Co., 1957.

These two inexpensive books about the general history of the Seminole Indians are available from the Great Outdoors Publishing Company, 4747 Twenty-eighth Street North, Saint Petersburg, Florida 33714.

Color Plates On Covers

Front cover. Backview of *Phoenix Rising* vest by Laura Munson Reinstatler. Collection of Virginia Avery. © 1985 Laura Munson Reinstatler.

Plate A. Back yoke and sleeve of dress that is often thought to be in Indian colors but is not. By the author.

Plate B. Skirt panel made of Ultrasuede patchwork. By Edith Carlson.

Plate C. Indian-made skirt, 1944.

Plate D. Indian-made shirt.

Plate E. Indian-made dolls.

Plate F. Broken Circle, 32 by 52 inches (81 by 132 cm.). Segments were cut at increasing angles and joined by spacers to repeat the same value range both vertically and horizontally. By Lassie Wittman.

Plate G. Indian-made. Owned by Frances Wood.

Plate H. Window Pane, 30 by 48 inches (76 by 122 cm.). Resembles a cottage window with a growing rose of Palestrina knots. By Flo Wilson Campbell.

Plate I. Indian-made dress. By Rosa Billie. Owned by Lassie Wittman.

Plate J. Contemporary sampler made by Mrs. Howard Osceola. Photo courtesy of Dorothy Downs.

Plate K. Indian-made bags.

Plate L. Detail of dress shown in Figs. 150 and 189. By Jane Lang Axtell.

Plate M. By Lassie Wittman, 1990.

Plate N. By Lassie Wittman.

Plate O. By Lassie Wittman.

Plate P. By Lassie Wittman.

Plate Q. Bird Plumage, 45 by 60 inches (114 by 152 cm.), by Flo Wilson Campbell.

Photo Credits

References are to figure number. All photographs are by author unless otherwise indicated.

Jean Affleck: 14, 154. Jane Lang Axtell: 148, 150, 167, 188–193, color plate L. Helen Bitar: 134. Janet Bryan: 9. Julie Goetsch: 144. Historical Museum of Southern Florida: 171. Hazel Hynds: 199. Michael James: 136. Margot Strand Jensen: 132. Gerry Machovec: 42, 206–214, 219, 220. Heather Price: 169. Patricia Rush: color plates M and N. Helen Russell: 168. Joy Saville: 187. Smithsonian Institution: 170 (photo 45–112F). Carol Tate: 34. Maggie Turner: 125, 135. Ken Wagner: color plate O. John Young: 121, 133, 139–141.

Index